<u>Endless</u>

By

Fireman Dave McFadden

Cover design by Karen M. McFadden
Artwork by Gavin L. McFadden

Love,
Fireman
Dave

9/21/17

The Author would like to thank first and foremost the God of Abraham, Issac, and Jacob for without Him this book would not be possible. To my mother Emily who introduced me to the Lord and wished nothing more than I would follow Him throughout all of my days. To my wife Karen and all of our children for putting up with me. To "Jelly" for all the prodding. To Sierra and her family for all of the support and guidance. Without all of you this book endeavor would not have been possible.

The Endless Miracles of God

Matthew

Matthew, our middle son, was only about seven months old when we began to notice that he was able to eat just fine; unfortunately he was not able to go number two. He would cry relentlessly and did what I commonly referred to as "pushing tears" from his eyes. We would walk the floor all night hoping he could go. We seldom found relief. We took him to the doctor and they asked us if he was vomiting. When we told them yes, they asked us if he was just spitting up or was it "projectile" vomiting. My first question was, "what?"

Projectile vomiting is when they throw up on one side of the room and it carries all the way over to the next wall. I told the doctor that he was doing just that. The doctor said he may be suffering from pyloric valve stenosis. The doctor said in about a week or so he would schedule some tests and then schedule Matthew for surgery. During that two week wait he continually got worse. We were going out of our minds. He was in so much pain.

A few days before the tests were to begin a friend of mine told me about a church service at a local church and he invited us to go. When we got there we met Pastor Carlos Lucina. After some opening remarks Pastor Lucina asked if anyone had a special need or just wanted to come up for prayer. I grabbed Matthew out of his mother's hands and I ran up to the altar where Pastor was standing.

Pastor told me to hold onto him, and then he laid hands on him and said, "Father, in the name of Jesus I ask that you touch this little child right now." The moment he made that petition, I felt Matthew squirm and he began to go so bad that he squirted out every side of that diaper. I had never seen a diaper so full in my life. From that day forward he never had another issue with pyloric valve stenosis.

The Car Fire

In August of 1967 I turned 6 years old. That November I went up north for the first time with my dad for the Michigan white tail deer hunting season. About half way on I-75 there is a gas station/store that is a regular stopping place for many northbound travelers. We call it Birch Run!

Back then it was just a large room with vending machines covering every inch of the inside walls. There were a few tables in the center of the room if the travelers wanted to sit and eat their food. I remember getting malted milk balls and a cold Mt. Dew. On that first trip I never had any inkling that this would become a family tradition that is still practiced today.

The Conlee Travel center today is a sprawling store, gas station, ice cream shop, and service center. It sits on the same location but is much different than my first experience back in 1967. Several years ago my wife and I and our three boys did our usual stop, and for me it was my goal to get my malted milk balls and a cold Mt. Dew. We were on our way home and it was about six o'clock in the evening when we got there.

As I pulled in there was only one other car parked out front and I parked two spaces away from it and we all went inside for our goodies. As I walked in I noticed a young girl looking her car over. I was not sure if she was having trouble with it or not. Once inside the boys scattered to search for their goodies and to go to the bathroom. Their mother did likewise. I, for the first time, did not even make a run for my coveted malted milk balls and never sought out a Mt. Dew. For whatever reason there was no desire to keep with my tradition.

I walked the entire store over two times and simply could not think of one thing that I wanted. My boys were so worried about me they asked their mom if I was ok. After not seeing anything that I wanted I did something that I had never done before. I walked over to the fountain drink machine and I got the largest glass of ice water that they offered. Now my boys were freaking out because I do not drink water, especially at Birch Run!

After we paid for our stuff we went outside to leave. As I walked out of the door I noticed that the car parked next to us was being attended by that same girl and this time she had the hood up. She was looking very intently over the motor and as I walked up she just stepped back about five feet. As I got up to the car to see if I could help her, the entire engine compartment exploded into a fire ball about ten feet in diameter. Without even thinking about what to do I threw that 48 ounce glass of ice water on the fire.

That small amount of ice water completely put the fire out. I knew right then why that I had no desire to get a Mt. Dew and some malted milk balls.

About 15 people witnessed this "miracle" that day. I stood there in awe because I am a professional firefighter and have a college degree in fire science and know for a fact that what I just saw and did was impossible except that God was in the works!

As the smoke cleared I checked the girl to see if she was ok, and she was, except for being scared by the explosion. I then turned my attention to the car and the motor. I made some very interesting observations. I told her that the insulation on the underside of the hood was not burnt or even singed. I also noticed that there was no burn residue on the motor. There was no damage to the engine compartment at all. As God began to deal with me about the whole situation I turned my attention to the girl.

She was young and very pretty! She was dressed up to the hilt and looked like she was going out for a fancy night on the town. I asked her name and then I told her about myself and my background in the Fire and EMS career. I also told her that without Godly intervention there was no way what just happened should have happened. I told her that a car fire of that magnitude would normally take between 500 and 750 gallons of water to put out. She witnessed, along with about 15 other people, that I did it with a glass of ice water. I then told her that it was no coincidence that I was there.

As I went on I told her about my insatiable desire to have a cold Mt. Dew and some malted milk balls. I told her that in my 25 years of Fire and EMS service that I had never encountered such a serious situation for the sole purpose of saving a life in this manner. I then asked her where she was going all dressed up. She told me that it was her 21st birthday and that a bunch of her girlfriends were taking her out to get her smashed. She said that she had never drunk alcohol and that her girlfriends promised to show her how it was done.

I began to make a summation of the events and occurrences that led us up to this car fire and I asked her if she felt that one bit of it was a chance happening. She said no! I told her that I believed with all of my heart that God put me there in order to preserve her life. I told her that her soul was in the balance and that I felt that if she continued on and went drinking with her friends that she may not live to tell about it the next day. As she listened intently to my words, others in the crowd that had gathered to see what had happened agreed with me. She then asked me what she should do. I told her that she may want to think seriously about going home.

As she stood there for a moment contemplating everything that had happened I told her to go home, slip into some comfortable clothes, put on a good movie, make some popcorn, and have a safe and quiet evening at home. I believed that I had done and said everything that God had placed in my heart to tell her. I closed the hood of her car and she hugged me. The car started and she drove away. I don't know if she went home or not but I believe that she did. I hope I never forget that day and that cup of ice water!

The Cave In

I think many were skeptical when my Uncle Fred sold everything in Monroe and moved to a place called Greasy Creek, Kentucky. Soon he was coal mining and not doing too bad for himself. Over the summer between my eighth grade year and my freshman year of high school my mom and dad decided that we would move to Kentucky and work with my Uncle. It wasn't long after we arrived that I was deep in the coal mines working. It was a great experience for me.

It is interesting when I tell people that I have worked in the coal mines of Kentucky. I always get that deer in the headlights look but the experience is none the less true. My dad, older brother, younger brother, and I all worked side by side inside the coal mines. We drilled the holes for the dynamite and then loaded the charges. We would all stand back as the words "Fire in the hole" were shouted. Soon we would hear a low rumble and then we would begin to shovel the coal out into the wheelbarrows. We would then walk behind the wheelbarrows and dump the coal into the truck waiting outside the mine. It was hard work but as kids we didn't see it that way.

Coal is usually found in what is called seams between rock and shale or slate. Only the coal brings money to the miners, so care had to be taken when setting off the charges. One day we set off the charges and a seam of coal about 4 feet thick fell to the ground but the seam of slate stayed intact on the ceiling of the mine. We then readied ourselves to shovel out the coal. As we started to shovel the coal a seam of slate rock about 4 feet thick came crashing down on us. As the smoke and dust cleared we all made it out except my younger brother Bill. He was trapped under 4 feet of slate rock. We now had a serious life safety threat with little time to act.

As we scurried to begin digging him out I made a startling discovery. The seam of slate rock broke right over him and actually acting like a protective gable roof I was able to grab him, and pull him to safety. He had landed on the loose coal which also aided in my ability to get him clear. I only worked in the coal mines for about six months and had seen many seams of slate and shale fall and never once experienced it where it fell and broke in two pieces. He never worked in the mines again. I think it was two fold. One was that my mom wouldn't let him back inside the mines and I think a bit of fear also took him over. Either way I know for a fact that he was spared that day!

JR

My brother-in-law has always been a big eater. I have said for years that the only way that JR stops eating is if you run out of money or you just leave the restaurant. The call came and news was spread that he was in the University of Michigan Hospital in Ann Arbor. He had been diagnosed with serious ulcerations to his stomach and esophagus. He had not had a bite to eat or nothing to drink in 6 weeks. Needless to say he lost a fair bit of weight. Thursday my wife told me that the doctors had said that they have done all they can do for him and one more test would be done the following Monday, and then the next day he would have his entire stomach removed. This would mean that he would be tube fed for the rest of his life. We were all saddened by this news.

On that Sunday following the news of his condition I stood up at church and quickly told everybody the story of JR. I then asked if I could stand in for him and have the entire church body come forward and circle around me and pray that God would hear our prayer and that JR could be healed. Tears filled my eyes as I looked and every seat was empty as everybody made their way up around the altar to pray for JR. As hands were joined, many began to petition the God of Abraham, Isaac, and Jacob. Soon everyone was praying. After a few minutes of prayer the entire body shouted "AMEN." It was a great feeling to come together in one mind and one accord for a person in need.

The next day the doctors in Ann Arbor did a test just to see how bad his ulcers were, and the doctors told my mother-in-law that his stomach was completely whole and that she could take him home right then. In about an hour the discharge papers were complete and according to JR's wishes he went straight to Wendy's for a double cheese everything meal. As of this date he has never had another issue with his stomach.

The Smashed Fingers

My wife had worked very hard to finish Radiology school and it was decided that we would go to Peppina's Restaurant in Lincoln Park to celebrate. Since I work 24 hour shifts as a Paramedic and a Firefighter it would be necessary for me to get my shift covered. I tried to take a vacation day but that got denied. I tried to trade my shift and nobody was available to cover for me.

I tried and tried all day to find somebody to no avail. All I said after my failed attempts was, "Lord, make a way for me to go please!" My wife's mother lived out of town and they were scheduled to arrive in Monroe around 5 pm and plans were to head to Lincoln Park at that time. As the day went by my chances of getting to go grew slimmer. I was bummed out.

At 3:10 pm a three car accident came in at the North Junction and we responded. We would soon learn that we only had one bad patient and she was suffering from chest pains. As we prepared to remove her from the car someone slammed the rear driver's door on her car and my index, middle, ring, and pinky finger got slammed in the door. My entire pinky finger, 3/4 of my ring finger, 2/3 of my middle finger, and 1/3 of my index finger was caught in the door. Since the door closed completely I could not get free.

With all of the noise of the traffic and fire trucks and ambulances nobody could hear me screaming. I was trying to pull my hand free and it would not release. Captain Carl Stanifer saw me flailing around in the door and was yelling out to me to see what was wrong. I kept yelling that my hand was caught and he finally saw it and he and another firefighter came to my rescue. When they got the door opened my fingers were smashed and red. They wrapped them up and took me to the ER.

By the time I got to the ER my fingers were red and starting to turn purple. My fingers were now swelling and I could not bend them very much. After being seen and treated by the ER doctor I was told that I would have to take the rest of the shift off and be seen first thing in the morning by the OHS doctor for a follow-up. I was taken back to my duty station and my arrival time back at the station was 4:50pm. My wife picked me up at 5pm and I got to go to her graduation celebration dinner. Even though my hand was wrapped up and I kept ice on it I was able to eat dinner. With help from pain meds I got through it just fine.

My appointment was at 8am the next morning with the OHS doctor. When I arrived the girls checked me in and I was put into a room.

When the doctor came in my hand was completely whole. He even asked me which hand was injured after viewing the right and the left. He looked at me with great amazement. He said, "This can't be possible!" He told me he read the night ER doctors report and said my hand should be black and blue and that I should not be able to move my fingers. He marveled at how my hand looked. He asked me if I was in any pain, especially when moving my fingers, and I told him no. He manipulated my hand and fingers and even read over the doctor's notes again from the day before. Finding nothing, he said I could return to work on my next scheduled shift!

Athlete's Foot

I'm not exactly certain where I caught it but I had the worst case of athlete's foot that I have ever had in my life. My feet were one big sore. I couldn't scratch them enough to get even a remote amount of relief. I knew that it would be church time soon and I pretty much had decided not to go. As the normal time for me to leave neared I made up my mind that God said he cared about me and my situations in life no matter how big or small. So I got ready and went to evening service.

As I walked into the church house many of the people there were staring at the way I walked. I was in pain and the itching was horrible. As service started Brother Delmar asked if anybody needed special prayer. I stood up and said that I did. Next to the altar is a special chair reserved for those who come in with a special need. As I sat down, some of the church members gathered around and before they prayed they asked me if it was my feet that were bothering me and I told them yes. I told them that I had a horrible case of athlete's foot. Without even a glitch they anointed my feet with oil and began to earnestly pray. After the prayer I got up and walked back to my seat. When I got back to my seat I pulled both of my socks off and my feet were completely healed. Even in this, God heard our prayer and healed me.

Ford Lake

It was around 5am on that morning and my mom was sleeping at home in Monroe. Being awakened by the spirit of God she was led by the spirit of God to pray for my wife Rose and her family. Being obedient to the calling she began to pray by her bedside. About 6 miles away in a small subdivision known as Detroit Beach the, Reverend Delmar Moore was also visited by the same spirit of God, and he too was told to pray for Rose and her family. Like my mother, and not knowing why, Brother Delmar slid out of his bed onto the floor and began praying for Rose and her family.

Just a few minutes after they started praying a full blown tornado hit the condos on Ford Lake in Ypsilanti, Michigan, some 35 miles away. My wife's mother and her husband lay sleeping unawares that a tornado would hit their condo. They both escaped unharmed. Dr. John W. Freud, a local OB/GYN and I were two of the first to get to tour the disaster site. His Aunt also lived on the third floor next door to my mother-in-law and her husband. As we toured the site we couldn't believe the damage.

As we went up to the third floor we were able to go inside my mother-in-law's apartment. The majority of the roof was lifted off their apartment and it rested over 50 feet away from their building in a parking lot. As I looked around I couldn't believe my eyes. Was it the damage that caught my eyes? No, moreover it was the lack thereof that was so unbelievable! I noticed that there were two birthday cards still standing on a dresser. As I looked up there was no roof! I thought to myself: how in the world can a tornado cause so much destruction to the roof of a building and leave birthday cards standing on the bedroom dresser?

I went over to a chest of drawers and there was a stack of one dollar bills that appeared as if they had not felt even a slight breeze. They were still sitting there untouched. In the entire room I noticed one piece of ceiling drywall about the size of a paper plate sitting on the foot of the bed. How extraordinary! Papers, clothes, nick knacks, and many other items were not out of their place and to my great surprise they were dry. When the storm came through it brought rain and hail yet not one drop of water was found in "THAT" apartment. As Dr. Freud and I surveyed the damage we were both speechless. He was a retired Army Captain and I had been in the Fire and EMS career for over 25 years and neither one of us had seen such unbelievable sights. Neither of my in-laws suffered any injuries.

Pepsi

When our boys were little and we were struggling along, we pooled together our pennies many times to get milk money. One day in particular my wife told me that we needed some ham from the Villa Party store for supper. So we all started digging for change and I headed out the door. As I got to my van I heard my wife say, "Would really be nice to have some Pepsi too!" I knew that I only had enough to buy a pound of sliced ham but I also knew that God was good and that He cared about me and my family. On the way to the store I searched my mind to determine if I had any other money stashed in the car. I soon realized that I did not! I knew though as God dealt with me that I would bring home a two liter of Pepsi.

I got to the store and went in and spent every dime that I had on the ham. Other than the owner and his wife I was the only customer. I thanked them and walked out of the store. As I got to my van I heard that very familiar sound of air brakes as the park brake on a semi truck is set. As I looked over it was a Pepsi truck driven by a very good friend of mine Dwight Redmon.

I looked over at him and he had a big smile on his face. I never said a word about wanting Pepsi. As he started to open the big sliding doors on the truck he made his way around to the other side. There on the passenger side was a very narrow door. As we stood there and chatted he looked at me and asked me if I knew the reason for the smaller door. I told him that I did not have a clue. He said that inside the smaller door was the two liters of Pepsi that he is allowed to give away. As I looked up he was handing me 2 two liters of Pepsi. When I got home I told my wife that I knew that God would make a way.

Tasha

Word came that Don and Jan were expecting and we were all glad at the news. It was soon though that we would get bad news that while still developing in her mother's womb that Tasha had developed a brain tumor the size of a lemon. They were truly upset. I got the call from my wife and it was a Wednesday. I told them that on Sunday that I would have special prayer for them all. Sunday came and I again called for the entire church to come forward so that we could go before God in prayer on behalf of this unborn child. Every seat in the house was empty.

We asked one of the women to stand in for Tasha and we all circled together and held hands. Soon a multitude of prayers was being sent up to heaven in hopes that God would hear our petition. The next day Jan had another ultra sound and the tumor the size of the lemon was gone. Tasha is now over 19 years old and has had no ill effects from that tumor at any time in her life.

The Picture Proof

After her visit, her OB/GYN doctor told her that she had advanced stages of endometrioses and that he would try some medication to see if he could get it under control. Medicine would soon prove fruitless, so her doctor required another office visit. He told her that he wanted to do a laparoscopy in surgery at our local hospital to see how serious the condition was. At the hospital her doctor told us that if the condition was as bad as he thought that it might be that he would probably have to do a full hysterectomy. She was then prepped for the procedure. Before they came in to take her down to surgery we asked the nurse if we could have prayer with her.

As we gathered around her bed we joined hands and began to pray and to ask the Lord to be with her in surgery. We asked God to touch her and heal her. At the end of the prayer the nurse told us that she would be in surgery for about 45 minutes and then off to recovery. We watched as she and the nurse disappeared through the doors of surgery.

About 15 minutes later her Doctor came to the waiting room and he was holding about 5 pictures. He called me over to where he was in the doorway of the surgery waiting room and told me that he had no idea what happened but the pictures he had showed a perfectly healthy womb. He then told me she had the womb of a 12 year old girl. He said, "I can't explain it!" She will be out of recovery in a bit and she can go home. Well, thank the LORD!

Maggie

It was getting to be about that time and the boys' mother should be home. It was a good sight to see that it was now 4:30 in the afternoon because I was really hungry. The boys told me that they were really hungry too and that when mom got home from work that we needed to go out to eat. The phone rang and it was my wife. She said that a really bad car accident had happened and that four serious patients were brought to the ER and that she would be tied up for a while doing their x-rays. We told her ok and that we would see her soon.

At about 5:00 she called back and said that she would be longer than she first had expected and that we could go and eat. I told her no and that we would wait for her. She hung up and went back to her patients. I decided that I would go out on the front porch and when I did my neighbor Maggie was sitting on her porch with her head hung down. As I looked intently at her God began to deal with me and told me to get my guitar and go over and sit with her. I laughed! I had just started playing the guitar and could only play two cords and they sounded pathetic. I went back inside the house.

Again, the phone rang and it was my wife telling me that she was trying to hurry but they were swamped with car accident victims. I assured her that it was ok and it was back to work for her. I stood there not able to get that sad look off of my mind that Maggie had so I went back out onto my porch. She was still sitting there and as soon as I saw her God began to deal with me again and told me to get my guitar and go over and talk to her. This time I gave in to God and I went and got my guitar and walked over and sat down next to her. As we sat there neither of us spoke a word.

I could literally feel the pain and hurt that she was experiencing! Her face was care worn and there was a great emptiness that emanated from her. As I sat there I had no idea what to say, do, or think. Like a small breeze of relief I felt the Holy Spirit of God come over me and God said sing "Prayer Bells of Heaven." Found on page 276 in the old country red Church Hymnal it was surely what was needed. I just started singing it out loud and my fingers moved gracefully over the cords of that guitar. I started out in the second verse and then went to the first and then the third and did it all over again. Maggie's house was right on the corner of a major intersection and most of the time the traffic noise was deafening but on this date and time the only thing you could hear was me singing that song. For over a half an hour I just kept singing that song again and again and again!

I never felt led of the Lord to sing anything but "Prayer Bells of Heaven." It wasn't long and that entire porch and front yard area was just gleaming as the spirit of the Lord flooded that space. A great relief and peace came over me and Maggie's countenance changed. With tears of joy in my eyes and tears of joy in her eyes, I stopped playing and singing and asked her if she was ok. She said, "Now I am!"

Maggie told me that she had decided to end her life that day. She said that she came out on the porch and was getting ready to go over to the Roessler Street Bridge and jump off into the waters below. She said, "I am so glad that you came over to sing and play for me." I then apologized about my playing ability and she said that it sounded just fine. She again thanked me. I told her that she was welcome and I told her that I loved her. As I began to get up she grabbed my arm and asked me to sit back down because there was something important that she wanted to tell me.

As I sat back down she said that she wanted to know why I picked "Prayer Bells of Heaven" as the song that I sang. I told her that I didn't, God did. As she sat there she just cried. I again told her that I was sorry for the way it must have sounded and she cried all the more. She then said to me, "You don't understand. When I was growing up as a little girl and any trouble or problems came our way, my mom would sing that same song over and over again until God brought an answer of peace. There is no way that you could have known that and what you did today brought me peace in spite of my troubles." She said that she was not going to hurt herself or jump off the bridge. I now play a little better than I did back then and I have probably sang that song more than a hundred times. It was, however, on that day that that song really came to life for me because it was mingled with the spirit of God and delivered right on time.

Tori Tori Tori

Dale and Bev had moved from the Upper Peninsula to Monroe and were living in an apartment complex about a mile south of my fire station. One morning I had decided to stop and see Dale about something and as I pulled out of the fire station I remembered that Dale was not home because he was at work. The thought of stopping left me and I continued to drive home. About half way there the thought entered my mind again to stop and see Dale. I discounted the thought again because I knew that he would not be there. As I continued the drive I came close to the apartment building and as soon as I saw the building the idea of stopping took me over and I pulled into the lot.

They lived on the third floor around towards the back. As I pulled up near the entrance door I saw the spot where Dale always parked and the truck was not there. I theorized that he was at work. As I sat there in my car I kept thinking that if his truck is not here and I know he is at work then why am I going in. God does move in mysterious ways!!

After convincing myself to go in I got out of my car and headed for the three flights of stairs that I would have to walk. As soon as I opened the main outside door I heard a loud scream, "Tori, Tori, Tori." That blood curdling scream was Bev and you could hear her from one end of that apartment complex to the other. It seemed as if I only hit about five steps on my way up to that apartment. As I got there the door was open and Bev was still screaming "Tori, Tori, Tori." I made my way in and ran to the bathroom and there was Bev holding her daughter Victoria (aka Tori).

Tori was being held by her mother in the sitting position on the bathroom sink. She was blue in the face and not breathing. Bev was screaming and shaking her for all she was worth. I immediately grabbed Tori and pushed Bev back out of the way. I laid Tori over the length of my arm and hit her right between the shoulder blades of her back. When I did this a large piece of hard candy came out of Tori's mouth and circled the bathroom sink several times before coming to a stop. Tori took a breath that seemed as if it would never end and she started to cry. What a welcomed sound that was. She got her color back and in minutes was fine.

Victoria is now a grown woman with kids of her own. We still talk about that day and time when God led me to this home, a panicked mother, and a choking baby. It has been over twenty years ago that this happened and I can still hear that hard piece of candy tinkling around in that sink.

The Roll Over

It was early that Saturday morning and for no apparent reason I drove into the city of Monroe. I lived in LaSalle so there was no purpose for me to be driving out to the beach areas. I came down North Monroe Street and made a right turn onto Noble Avenue. As I drove east towards North Dixie Highway I noticed a car that had driven through the T-shaped intersection and was rolled over next to the utility pole. I didn't see anyone around the car so my first thought was that it was merely a property damaged accident. As I began to turn to go north onto North Dixie Highway, I thought I saw a person lying on the ground so I stopped my car and went over to investigate. As I walked around the car I noticed a young girl on her back not breathing. She had been partially ejected from the car.

She lay there motionless as I made the observation that she was not breathing. Her face was ashen grey from the lack of oxygen. Fearing a neck injury I had to do a maneuver that allows for the airway to be opened and not cause any damage to the neck. As I opened the airway with the Jaw-Thrust Maneuver she started to breathe again on her own. Soon I could hear the sound of sirens as I knew that help was on the way. I stayed with that girl until the Paramedics loaded her into the back of the ambulance. She was only 16 years old.

Once at Mercy Hospital the Emergency Room Doctor told the family that she probably would have died right there under her car if I would not have come along. My only answer is but for the grace of God that girl would have probably died right there. By His love and mercy I was able to be a part of saving a young girls life. To God be the glory!

Emma

A minor bout with abdominal pain prompted a visit to the family doctor. That visit and a few X-rays brought on a visit to our local surgeon. As I sat there with my mom the surgeon carefully looked over the x-rays and CAT scan films and then the doctor turned and looked at my mom and said, "Emma, you have an abdominal aneurysm!" I don't think that she had a clue what he was saying but I surely did. He then went on to explain that this is a weak spot in an artery that runs down the length of the body. He said it was 7 cm long and just above the junction of the renal artery. He smiled and said, "Well, I was looking for a hernia and found an aneurysm."

Not sure what all the hub bub was about, the doctor sat down and explained in detail the significance of finding this aneurysm and what his recommendations were. He recommended a specialist in Ann Arbor at the U of M Medical center and she made an appointment. In just a few days we were in Ann Arbor and got the news from the specialist that she would need surgery to fix the problem. The date was set.

All of my mother's children are in the medical field but one. The oldest, Dr. Martin A. McFadden, is a U of M doctor. I am a Paramedic and a Firefighter. Lori A.

(McFadden) Miracle is a CT/MRI Technician and the youngest sister Melissa D. (McFadden) Horrigan is an RN. My brother Billy R. McFadden is a lineman for DTE. As we talked with the specialist we were able to understand the risks and serious complications associated with an aneurysm, the treatment, and follow up considerations. After talking with the specialist the surgery date was set.

Most of us knowing all too well that this weak spot in her artery could be fatal we were justly concerned. We are also acutely aware that we serve a God that is greater than any aneurysm! So they came and took Emma back to her little cubicle area for her surgery prep. There were no walls in this very large room. Each patient and their family were separated by cloth curtains. In the center of this large room was a large work station that was buzzing with activity. Along each of the four walls there were these cubicles and in every one of them were a patient and their family members. Needless to say, the room was packed out with at least 100 people including medical staff, patients, and their families.

The surgeon met with us one last time before he left to prepare for the surgery. He said," I need to tell you some important things." He said, "When mom comes out of surgery she will be in serious condition!"

"She will have a breathing tube in her throat and will not be responsive. She will be taken to the ICU and will probably be there for several days. After that she will be in a step-down ICU and then she will go to a Med-Surg floor until she is ready to go home. This is a very serious surgery and I just want to prepare you for what condition she will be in after surgery." We all acknowledged his concerns and he left.

As the nurse came into our cubicle she told us that she would be going down to surgery soon and that everybody should visit for just a minute and then proceed to the waiting room. Each of those that were there took their turn to be with Emma for just a minute and then they returned to the waiting room. The last to visit was me, my youngest son Mark, and my nephew Jared. As we stood there God's spirit moved over me with a song!

I looked at Mark and Jared and I said, "Alright guys strike up a tune!" Without any accompanying music Mark and Jared began to sing the old song, "The Hem of His Garment." It goes like this:

A Woman one day tried many physicians,

But only grew worse in the Bible we're told.

But when she heard she came unto Jesus,

She found what she needed for body and soul!

Chorus

If I could just touch the hem of His garment.

If I could just touch one part of His clothes.

I know I'd be healed, my sins all forgiven.

If I could just touch Him I know I'd be whole.

Mark and Jared were in perfect harmony and the spirit of God began to fill that large room as they sang. The front curtain was open and as I looked out around the large room I observed a very profound sight. Everyone in there stopped what they were doing! Everybody stopped talking and the family members made their way to the opening of their individual cubicles. During the time that they sang the phones never rang and not one person left the room and not one person came into the room. With the exception of them singing you could have heard a pin drop a hundred yards away.

As the mighty power of God moved around that room a healing was in the air. The people just stood there in awe. When the song was finished we had prayer with my mom and we left to go to the waiting room.

Not one person said a word as we walked out. They took Emma down for surgery and the time of our vigil began. They said it would take several hours.

As we sat there waiting we decided that only a few of us would go into recovery to see her when the surgery was done. After many hours the nurse came in and told us that one of us could go down and see her. Since my sister Lori worked for the U of M it was decided that she would go in first. After several minutes I looked down the long hallway leading to the recovery room and here came my sister with a quick gait making her way to the waiting room. I profoundly remember as she walked that the bottom of her long lab coat flapped in the air generated from her fast walking. Lori, as she got to the waiting room, just pointed back over her shoulder with a fist made and her thumb pointing the way said, "You better go see her!"

When I entered the room I did not see her. All the way over to the other side of the room is where the patients go in for surgery. All I saw was one bed with a patient sitting up about half way with only an IV pole next to her. My first thought was that couldn't be her because her doctor said she would be on a ventilator machine with all kind of gadgets hanging off of her. My second thought was that they usually do not bring post-op patients into the patient pre-op area. Nothing at this time was making any sense! Seeing no other patients I decided that I would walk across that big room to see if I could find her.

As I approached that lone bed near the entry door "TO" surgery I recognized that face and that smile. I said, "Emma?" My mom looked as if she had not even had a mole removed! She was sitting up talking to me as if she had never had surgery at all. I asked, "How are you feeling?" She said, "Just fine!" Then I heard those words that let me know that she was ultimately ok. She looked at me and said, "I could really use a cigarette and a cup of coffee." Even though she looked awesome they still took her to the ICU. Her doctor saw me standing there and as they took her away he had the most peculiar look on his face. He said, "Mr. McFadden, in over three decades of being a surgeon and considering her condition; I have never seen anything like this in my life." I said, "Thank the Lord!"

They put her in the ICU and after about three days of that she told the doctor that she was tired of sitting around doing nothing. What normally amounts to about seven to ten days of post-op hospitalization only lasted four days. To this date there has not been one hint of a problem from that surgery.

In the New Testament in the Bible the story of the woman with a medical condition is captured in the book of St. Mark chapter 5 verses 25 through 29. She had done all that she could to be healed. One day she heard that Jesus was passing by. She reasoned within herself that if she could just reach down and touch the hem of his robe that she would be healed. This great story about faith was the basis for the song that Mark and Jared sang. Everybody in that room during pre-op heard the singing and the spirit of God was thick enough to cut with a chain saw. Just as important was the fact that after surgery they brought her back into the same room where those same people could personally see the mighty works that the Lord performed that day.

As the days went by she was the talk of the town in the ICU. The nurses and the other staff could not get over the fact that this great miracle had been performed for her. After several days the specialist let her go home!

The Back Pain

   I have had several times when my back would hurt but this time I was down for the count. I had never experienced a problem that left me unable to even get up out of bed. I was in serious pain. Knowing the power of God and knowing that when Jesus was beaten it was for our healing (Isaiah Chapter 53) and our better health, I called Brother Delmar. Reverend Delmar Moore is the Pastor of Grace Missionary Baptist Church in Monroe and he is a firm believer in the Lord healing people. As I lay there I kept thinking that I would call him to see if he would pray with me.

   Hearing some commotion down in the living room I yelled to my wife to see who had come in the door. It was a friend of hers and soon my wife came up the stairs. She said that she and her friend were going to go for a walk and that our three boys would keep an eye on me. I was literally unable to even sit up in bed. As she got ready to leave I asked her to set the phone near me in case I needed to make a call. She set the phone down and left. After about five minutes I couldn't take it any more so I called Brother Delmar.

   As we talked on the phone I began to tell Brother Delmar about my back and I told him how bad that it had gotten.

No matter what I did I had no relief. I asked him to give me 5 minutes and then start praying for me. He then asked me why the five minutes. I told him that it would take me five minutes to pull myself out of the bed and onto the floor. I then said that I would drag myself to the bathroom and since the bathroom was next to my bedroom I figured it would take about 5 minutes. I told him that I would pray with him and agree with him that God would touch me and that my back pain would go away. He said ok and I hung up the phone.

Even though I could hardly stand it I pulled myself onto the floor. I then started to crawl towards the bathroom. About half way I just stood up. I didn't know what to think because we had not even prayed yet. All I knew was that my pain was gone and all of the stiffness in my back was gone. I walked into the bedroom and called Brother Delmar to tell him what happened. When I started to tell him he just said, "I already knew!" I asked him, "Knew what?" He said that as soon as we hung up the phone that he started praying. He said that the Bible says that God will answer our prayers even before we ask Him. He truly did because I did not even make it to the bathroom let alone start to pray. I thanked Brother Delmar and then I "ran" down the road towards my wife and her friend to tell them the good news!

Tracy

My phone rang and my secretary asked me if I had an intake patient scheduled. I told her no and she said that I had a woman at the front office needing to detox. I went to the office and when I came around the corner I saw a woman in her mid forties that looked as close to death as any person that I had seen in over three decades of working in the EMS career. Her family was distraught and said that if we did not help her that she would probably die. I wholeheartedly agreed.

We went to the intake office and as she sat across from me I could feel her desperation. She was very thin and her skin was extremely pale. She was having pains all over her body and did not even know the last time that she had eaten. We talked for hours as I did her intake paperwork. She shared with me pretty much her life's story about her addiction and about all of the great and wonderful things that she once had but lost due to drug use. She talked about her kids and about all of the sadness and hurts that she had experienced over the years. As we talked I just felt as if she may not live through the night.

After the intake paperwork was done I told her that she may want to go and try and sleep. She told me that she had not slept one night through in 15 years. She said she couldn't sleep due to the drugs, endless paranoia from being an addict and a drug dealer, and always being on edge. It was at this time that I began to tell her about the Lord. Not religious gibberish moreover I just told her how that Jesus loved her and that He cared. I told her that I thought that she could surely die during the night without Godly intervention. She went on to say that she knew God and that He cared. I told her though that it was this night that I would pray that God would reveal Himself to her in such a way that she would never forget it and that there would be no mistake that God had intervened and touched her.

She laid down at about 11:00 pm and all night long I kept a vigil outside her door praying that somehow God would deal with her heart. It was a long night because of her history but she never came out of the room. At about 7:00am she appeared in the doorway and if I would not have heard her voice I would have sworn that it was not the same person! She said to me as she opened the door that she fell fast asleep the minute her head hit the pillow and that she never moved an inch until she woke up at 7:00am. Truly a transformation took place that night and God definitely came to her rescue. She had a smile on her face and her countenance was one of peace.

As Tracy and I sat in my office talking another client came in and asked me if my detox client had bailed in the middle of the night. I asked the client as to why they felt that Tracy had bailed. She told me that nobody had seen her at breakfast and that the detox room was empty. With Tracy sitting right there next to her she did not even recognize her. Tracy looked at the other client and said, "I'm right here." The other client couldn't believe that it was the same person. Soon news went throughout the complex that Tracy was still here and that she even ate breakfast with many clients who had seen her the night before and they didn't even recognize her now.

Tracy wore mostly motorcycle laden t-shirts and black bandanas on her head. She looked like a "biker" chick. (Her confession) Although we talked about many things, the one thing that she missed the most was her kids. She cried as she talked about the regrets that she had concerning her children. As the thought came over me I told her that I had an idea. I told her that Mother's Day was just around the corner and that it was high time that her kids get to see their mommy again. I put the plan into action.

The first thing that needed to happen was a complete makeover. The girls at the center and I got the necessary items together to color her hair and to get it cut. They did her nails and her make-up. Next I went to church and told some of the women in the ladies group that I knew a woman in need of some clothing items. After getting Tracy's sizes the girls went and bought her a beautiful yellow sun dress with flowers on it. Next they picked out a beautiful pair of new shoes. They got her some other items and when she got herself all dressed up she looked like a princess. For the first time in 15 years she said she really felt like a real person again.

I take no credit for the work that God did that night. My joy comes from hearing her telling others the story of how an old hose head Paramedic told her about a man called Jesus. I relive that night when I hear her tell how she really thought she would die during the night and how she was rescued. I love to reminisce about the testimonies of those who did not even realize that they were testifying about the wonders of the God of Abraham, Isaac, and Jacob. She had an opportunity to see her children on Mother's Day and I wasn't able to be there but the sight of her must have been much more to be desired than the day that I first met a girl named Tracy.

"Go Back"

As I came out of the post office I noticed the burgundy car parked next to mine with the hood up. As I walked to my car I saw this middle aged woman looking down at her engine. She appeared to be wiggling the battery cables as I walked by. Not really feeling led to speak to her I just said, "Hi." I got into my car and began to drive off. The driveway to our post office in Monroe starts at the west side of the property and cars leave at the east end with the drive being only one way. As I drove to the end of the driveway I stopped my car and would have just drove on my way and God said, "Go back!"

I sat there for a second and said, "Go back?" God said again to me, "Go back!" So, I just drove back towards the west entrance and pulled back into the post office drive way and pulled back beside her car and got out. As I approached her car she was still fussing with her battery cables trying to get her car to start. As I walked up I asked her what was wrong and I asked if I could help. With a warm smile and a sigh of relief she just said, "Please!"

I looked at the battery and the cables were worn out and they were not connected very well. She said that sometimes if she just twists them around that she can get a connection and the car starts. As I continued to check out the battery I felt these eyes just staring at me. As I started to tell her to get in and try to start the car I looked up at her and her eyes were fixed on me and she had the most peculiar look on her face. She then said that she had a question for me.

She said, "When you came out of the post office you saw that I was broke down. As you got near to your car you looked over at me and said hi. You got into your car and left but I saw you sitting at the road for a minute and then you came back around and then asked me if I needed help." She then asked me, "Why did you come back?" I looked at her and said, "Can I tell you the truth as to why I came back?" And she said, "Yes!" I told her that God said, "Go back!" She asked, "He did?" I told her that when I first saw her that I did not feel led of the spirit of God to help. This was why that I went on my way. When I got to the edge of the road God told me to go back to help you and that is why I came back around.

She got into her car and as I wiggled the cable she turned the key and it started. With a sigh of relief she got out and I closed the hood. I told her that I did not believe for one minute that God sent me back for a bad battery. She agreed!

I then asked her if anything else was going on in her life that she needed help with from the Lord. As tears pooled into her eyes she said yes. I told her that I would help her if I could. She began to tell me how that the courts would soon decide if she would get to see her sons again. She told me that when she was a young mother that she was badly addicted to drugs and she went wild without a care in life. She said that she didn't mean to be that way but she just let drug abuse and drinking conquer her life. With the courts seeing little chance of a change in her life they took her kids and put them with foster parents.

The boys were just little back then, she went on to say, and that she missed them terribly. She was glad that they were in the care of foster parents but really wanted to see them. As she continued she told me that she had two very real and heartfelt fears. If the first one was not overcome then the second wouldn't matter. She said my first goal is to convince the court that I am now clean, working, and a responsible person. She said that is not the part that bothers me the most. I told her to say on!

She said that she has worked very hard to prove herself to the court and she felt that they would let her see the boys. As she started to cry more she then said, "But what if they don't want to see me!" She looked like she could just collapse and her crying got worse. She said that it seemed hopeless that she would get her boys to forgive her and to want her in their lives again. She leaned on me and I could tell that she felt as though all was but gone. She kept saying that it was an impossible thing for them to forgive her after all that she had done to them. As we stood there I told her that God does His best work in impossible situations.

I told her that she could count on me for help. I gave her my cell phone number and told her that anytime night or day that if she felt scared, alone, or that the situation was hopeless to call me. And she did! There were plenty of times that she would call me when she felt bad and I told her that I would pray that God would send His Holy Spirit to comfort her. I told her that God was a very present help in a time of trouble. I assured her that I would really take her and her sons on my heart and to seek God that He would make everything ok. And the court date approached!

When it was a few days before her hearing she began to tell me that she did not know if she could do this. I told her that in the name of Jesus that she could! I told her that I had been praying that God would take away all of the fear and anxiety so that she could boldly stand before the judge and not be afraid. She had her moments of jitters but I told her that now was the time to really trust that God was going to help her.

She went to court and when she called me she was already crying. She told me that the judge ruled that she had done what she said that she would do and that he felt as if she was sincere. He approved supervised visits with her boys and if those visits went well that he would address the matter again at a later date. He placed no restrictions on her and advised her to feel free to contact the foster parents and set up a reunion date. In all of her tears she told me that she was not scared at all anymore and that she was going to make that call that she had longed to make.

I spoke with her a few weeks later face to face and she just cried as she stood there hugging me. She kept thanking me for believing in her and praying for her throughout her ordeal. She said that her boys welcomed her with open arms and were really glad to see her. She said that for now the foster parents assured her that she could see them as much as she wanted and even agreed that as things progressed that she could have them for overnight stays and weekends.

As she thanked me I told her that I did not deserve the thanks. I told her that God did the work and that He deserved all of the credit. I told her again that when I came out of the post office that day that I truly had no real thoughts about helping her. I also told her that were it not for God's leadership that I would have just went on my way. I can honestly say that I thank the Lord for His goodness in this time in my life and I am glad that as I neared the road and would have just driven off He told me to….. "Go back!"

The Cross

I started to feel a really bad headache coming on and this time it was different than any other that I had felt. The pain was moving slowly down my neck and into the center of my back. As time went on I noticed that all of my joints started to stiffen and I was having trouble walking. As the days went by I really had trouble walking and my eyes were hurting me. I could hardly stand any light and it made my headache much worse. Soon I was hunched over and my joints were so stiff I could hardly move. My wife took me to the ER and I was treated for viral meningitis.

I was absolutely beside myself! My family said that I was hallucinating and talking out of my head. The pain was so intense it seemed unbearable. IV's, spinal taps, medications, and 24 hour care was in store for me for couple of weeks. I don't really remember much about the first week or so.

I was admitted into a private room and there was no light in the room. I was suffering from "Photophobia" and any flicker of light sent me reeling from pain. I am not sure how many days that I laid there in that dark room but all I remember was that I could hear people coming in and out but I didn't know who they were. I remember hearing their voices and seeing blurred visions of movement but that was it. The first morning that I woke up and could open my eyes to look around the room without it hurting, I looked at the wall that was at the foot of my bed. As my vision cleared I could see the shadow of a cross about four feet tall. I knew right then and there that God had truly visited me in my hour of need.

As I laid there looking at that cross I began to think about how good that God is to us and that He really cares. I was no longer in pain and my joints were not as stiff. As each day went by I would wake up in the morning and that same shadow of that cross was there. As soon as I was not photophobic anymore the nurses opened the blinds and the shadow of that cross was not seen by me again. Even though it was not there I knew that God was. I recovered from the meningitis and can honestly say that it was an experience for me and my family.

After I was released from the hospital I went home to convalesce for a few weeks. As family and friends visited me at my home they told me that they visited me at the hospital and had gotten a good laugh from watching me talking to people who weren't really there. Even though I was sick some of it was pretty funny. It was then that I got to tell them about that shadow of the cross that God had put on the wall for me to see each morning.

Tom Evans

As I came into the kitchen I noticed my patient was having a great deal of trouble breathing. On the other side of the kitchen table was a very tall slender man whose name was Tom. He was from Tennessee and was a very soft spoken country gent. Tom was trying to tell me about his friend's medical condition but it was very hard to understand him. Tom had surgery and his voice was very slurred making it difficult for me to understand what he was saying. We loaded our patient into the ambulance and he was taken to our local hospital for further evaluation.

It was about two weeks later and I had traveled to my sister's house in LaSalle, Michigan, and when I walked in there sat the same man that I had met a week earlier on that rescue call. When I saw him he smiled and said, "Hey, I know you!" As we both laughed I asked him how he knew my sister and her family. They had met through another friend of ours and then everybody in my sister's family adopted him. After we met we became friends too. He started going to church with us and every now and then he would sing an old country hymn. Tom was a very likeable and pleasant person to be in the company with.

As the years passed by we would get together and sing with Tom and go places. He had a nice home in Claiborne

County, Tennessee, and he would routinely let us go and stay there for vacation. He always had stories of the road and was always willing to lend a helping hand. He was the epitome of what a friend, mentor, and Christian Brother could be.

Word came one day that he was sick and was being tested for cancer. The results came back that would have caused most to lament or complain. Not Tom! In all things he would give God the praise and glory for it. He was admitted to our local hospital and while he was there most of the youth singers went to see him. After visiting with Tom for awhile the kids got together and started singing for him. There was no music accompaniment and their voices blended with great harmony. The Spirit of God filled that whole wing of the hospital as they sang the old songs of Zion. Tom loved to sing about the Lord and he loved it when others did too.

As we got ready to leave we wanted to have prayer with Tom. As we got ready to pray he pulled back the curtain of the gentleman in the bed beside him and asked him if he had any prayer requests. Tom then told him that we would remember him in prayer. As all heads were bowed everybody prayed for Tom and his roommate.

As the prayer ended we all hugged Tom and told his roomy goodbye. As we walked down the hallway people kept asking who the singers were. Tom always loved music, especially when it was spirit-filled music about the Lord.

My sister was the first to call me when she received news that Tom had went home to be with the Lord. He was very sure of his Christian faith and loved to share the good news of God's plan of salvation for mankind. He truly was not ashamed of his Lord. She told me that he would be shown locally here in Monroe at a funeral home and then he would be taken to another funeral home in New Tazewell, Tennessee. From there he would be buried in the Evans family cemetery in Lone Mountain, Tennessee.

That was a very hard pill for me to swallow because he was like a dad to me. I loved being in church with him and he loved being there with us. As funeral arrangements were made, the young Christians at our church were asked if we wanted to sing at his funeral. What a great privilege and honor I thought that would be. Now would be the hard part and that was picking the right song for the service. There were so many songs that Tom liked and I knew that I would seriously have to seek the face of God and then follow the leadership of the Lord. That's not always easy for me to do!

As I prayed and sought God about this, God laid the song, "Where the Roses Never Fade" on my heart. I can honestly say that I love that song. It was most certainly meant to be. I contacted the boys and told them about the song that God had laid on my heart and they all agreed that this would be the one. We got together and practiced it a few times and we readied ourselves for the funeral. We went to the funeral home here in Monroe for the local service, but we did not sing here. Our singing would be done in Tennessee. After the local service we headed for New Tazewell.

When we got to the funeral home in New Tazewell, the boys and I went to a back room to talk about our participation in the service. My guitar was tuned and we were ready to go. Just as we prepared to go into the parlor we decided to have prayer. We all wanted to know for sure that what we were planning to do and sing was what God wanted. Time came and we filed out of the back room down the main hallway to the room where the service was being conducted. As we stood there at the entrance we noticed a house full of friends and family that had gathered for the service.

As we started to walk in single file everyone in the funeral home was seated and the Pastor of the church was at the podium getting ready to start the service. I then noticed two women standing in the aisle about half way down to where the casket was sitting.

I did not know them and I had never seen them before. As we got to them we stopped and the one lady looked at the other and said, "Oh, these must be the singers from Michigan!" As they moved over to let us by the other lady said, "Wouldn't it be nice if they would sing "Where the Roses Never Fade!"

I just about jumped out of my skin! We didn't tell anyone what we were singing and except for Godly intervention we may not have ever sung that song. The service started and soon it was our turn to sing. As God's spirit moved throughout that funeral home we sang. After the service we found out that the two women were one of Tom's sisters and a friend of the family. His sister told us that Tom would have been delighted to know that we sung that song because it meant so much to him.

"No Turbulence Here"

My brother-in-law Dan and his wife Jean were looking to move back to Monroe from Texas. His tour in the Navy had ended and he wanted to come back home. My mother-in-law asked me if I would go to Texas and help them drive back to Monroe. Since I am scared to fly I asked, "Who is driving me to Texas?" My mother-in-law said that she had already bought my ticket to fly down and with great hesitation I agreed.

The flight from Detroit to Chicago seemed to go real nice. I was only white knuckled on the plane for 45 minutes. The part that was scaring me the most was that plane ride from Chicago to Houston. From there we would drive back to Monroe in a caravan of their car and a moving truck. I arrived in Chicago and paced the floor in an hour layover until I boarded my next nerve wrecking disaster. And the clocked ticked!

As we sat there on the runway I kept saying to myself over and over again, "I think I can, I think I can!" Soon the engines roared and we took off like a bullet. As I sat back in my seat all I could think of was that poor lady sitting directly in front of me who was probably going to get showered with my lunch. I felt the plane leave the ground and it started to ascend to a height of about 35,000 feet.

Soon we leveled off and I was not doing too badly. There were a few bumps but nothing that caused me any panic. Soon the Captain came over the intercom to tell us that we were flying at about 35,000 feet at a speed of about 600 miles an hour and that we could now take off our seat belts and move about the cabin. I thought "WOW" my preflight prayer was answered........kinda.

We weren't out of our seat belts 5 minutes when all of these lights started blinking and tones ringing and the Captain came back on the intercom to tell us to take our seats and to buckle up. He told us that the last 4 flights that went before us had hit some serious turbulence. He said that the flight just 20 minutes in front of us hit such violent winds that a cart was overturned and a flight attendant was injured. My life flashed before my eyes and I saw my lunch making its way back out of my body.

I did not know what to do. The flight attendants started securing their carts and they rushed around to get things secure before we hit the bad weather. The Captain came back over the intercom and told the flight attendants to take their seats. I was almost hyperventilating. As I neared panic I remembered who I was and who my trust and faith were secured in. I laid my head back and began to talk to God about my fears.

I said, "Lord, you know that I can't do this! I need your help and grace to carry me through this storm. I have no hope without your help and I need you to help me get through this bad time. Lord, I am asking you this in the name of Jesus." As soon as I ended this short but powerful prayer I fell fast asleep. Without the settling power of the spirit of God there is no way that I could have fallen asleep in this plane.

What seemed like an hour later I woke up and then looked around the plane. The plane was not bouncing around at all. Just then the Captain came over the intercom and said, "Well folks I am not sure what happened but we are on the exact same flight path as those planes that went before us. I tried to get above the storm but I am not sure how we went through the exact same storm cell and we did not have one moment of turbulence affect this plane. You are free to remove your seat belts and move about the cabin."

From that moment on we never bounced one time. We landed in Houston in record time and that without a glitch. I almost allowed fear to reign over me and to conquer me but I am glad I prayed. I thanked God for blessing me with such a great trip. I never really told that lady that sat in front of me how much danger that she was in but I guess some things are just better left unsaid!

Brother Mike Golden

It was freezing outside that night as I went out to start my Dodge Omni 4 door. I think it was about 11 degrees below zero wind chill. I was planning on leaving a bit early for class that night since it took about 45 minutes to get there. Owens Community College was just south of the Maumee River south of Toledo, Ohio, so it took a little while to get there. After the car warmed up I grabbed my books and headed out the door. I had no idea what a trip that this would turn out to be.

As I sped up to enter the freeway at South Otter Creek Road at Southbound I-75 the car began to lose speed and it stalled just as I entered the freeway. My first thought was, "Great! Now what do I do?" At this interchange there are just a few homes and some businesses that had already closed for the day. For me to walk to any one of them would have been a mile or more to walk in that open freezing weather. The car was warm so I just sat there wondering what to do. I did not have a cell phone so calling for help was not an option. I knew it wouldn't be long till I got cold.

After about 10 minutes I thought that I would try to start the car. I did and it started right up! I then thought that I would slowly back up the entrance ramp and then I could be home in less than 10 minutes. I put the car in reverse, checked my rear view mirror, and as I started to back up God began to deal with my heart and He said, "Keep going!" My first thought was I did not want to venture any more south on that freeway and it stall again. As I just sat there I began to ask the Lord if He was sure that He wanted me to continue to school or not. God said, "Yes!"

I cautiously entered the freeway and the car was running just fine so with little thought I continued on. As I crossed the Michigan Ohio border I neared Alexis Road and all of a sudden the car just stalled out. I tried to pull off the road as much as I could to avoid traffic. I was about 100 feet from the exit ramp to Alexis Road sitting, again, on the freeway. I had traveled about 8 miles and there I sat again wondering what in the world I was going to do. This time though it was a bit different. I was actually on the side of the freeway and as those semi trucks went past me it felt like I was a sparrow in a wind tunnel.

The car had been running enough to have plenty of heat inside but with that wind I knew it would be cold in there pretty soon. As I sat there I calculated that it would be at least a mile walk for help and that did not seem like such a likeable option. After 10 minutes I tried to start it again.

The car fired right back up...again! I thought that my luck may have run out so my first thought was to exit at Alexis and drive to the Pilot Truck Stop and call for help. Just as I headed for the exit ramp God said to me, "Keep going!"

As I slowly inched my way along the shoulder of the road I asked the Lord, "Are you sure?" God told me to keep going. I pulled out onto the freeway and gunned it and I was on my way again. I must have driven about 8 or 10 miles and, yes sports fans that's right, the car stalled again. This time I was near the exit to the Anthony Wayne Trail. Now I am near downtown Toledo and I just coasted off the side of the road. As semi trucks blasted by me I just kept thinking about how close to home that I was when the car first stalled. I just sat there thinking, "Lord, there must be a reason why that you keep telling me to keep on going." So I sat there....waiting....again!

After about 15 minutes I reached up to the keys, winced a bit and turned the ignition. The car started right up and I was again on my way. This was getting to be an interesting trip and God just kept telling me to keep going. I knew now that there was a good reason why He wanted me to continue. The reason for my God inspired determination hadn't been revealed just yet.

I was a bit worried because I had to cross the bridge over the Maumee River. It was about a mile long stretch and there was very little shoulder of the road for me to sit on. I have to say that I had thought about exiting before the bridge and to try and go back home but then I realized that God had brought me safe thus far so I just believed He would take me over the bridge. As the bridge came into view I just said, "Lord, please don't let me stall on this bridge!" I crossed the bridge just fine and took the next exit which was for the college. After I exited the freeway I continued to the school. I was about a half an hour late but I didn't care. As I pulled into my parking space it died and this time it made a low rumbling sound.

I decided that after class that I would call home from the school and have my wife make arrangements for someone to come and get me. After class I walked down to one of the payphones and as I started to dial the phone God said, "Keep going!" My first thought was that when I finally made it to the school, it sounded like something under the hood of my car had blown up. I didn't look under the hood but it sounded really bad. I headed to my car!

It had been snowing and my car was now covered with ice and snow. The wind was going right through me as I tried to scrape off the snow and ice. I got into the car, put the key in the ignition, and it started right up! After a few minutes it was defrosting and I was on my way.....sorta!

As I got onto Northbound I-75, I was now battling a headwind and more snow and ice. I just kept trudging north heading home. I got over the Maumee River Bridge but not by very much. The car stalled again and I pulled off the side of the road onto the shoulder. I was near the Bancroft Exit...sitting....again.

The car had enough time to warm up each time that I stalled out. This time was no different. After about 15 minutes I tried to start my car and she fired right up! I was on my way again. Each time it started I thanked God for His mercy. I continued north and was near the I-75 and I-280 interchange and it stalled again. It was off to the shoulder of the road again for my usual 15 minutes and ole Bessie would start again and I would be on my way. Each mile of the way I kept wondering why the Lord just kept instilling in me to just keep going. Up to this point I had no idea why.

As the car started I pulled back onto North bound I-75 and away I went. After I passed Alexis road I knew that the next 6 or 7 miles of the trip would be the most dangerous. At the Michigan and Ohio border heading north there are no exits with a gas station or other businesses. Until the

Luna Pier exit there are no homes readily accessible. This is a very long dark stretch of roadway. I just kept thinking about God telling me to keep going!

As I crossed the state line I looked way up ahead of me and I could barely make out these two yellow flashing emergency lights on the back of this car that was pulled over to the side of the road. They were hardly visible and they were blinking very slowly. I knew right then that this car has been off the road for awhile. As I got closer I could see where the snow had started to cover the rear and top side of the car. I couldn't tell if anyone was inside and thought that I would just "keep going" but God said to stop! I knew right then that there was a reason for me to keep going that night.

I pulled in front of the car and started to back up. As I looked in my mirror I could barely see as the passenger side door opened. I remember noticing that the battery must have been almost dead because the interior light of that car was real dim. As I stopped I could only see the silhouette of a person making their way to the passenger side of my car. I reached over and rolled down the window. I couldn't see if it was a man or woman and I couldn't make out their face. As the person got to my door I hear, "Brother Dave?" I thought, "I recognize that voice!" The man looked into the window and I said, "Brother Mike is that you?" And he said, "Yes it is!" I told him to get in. He said that he would go back to his car and get his wife. I think I heard him shout as he walked back to his car. It was not a shout from fear or anger but praise unto the Lord!

Brother Mike Golden and his wife had been to Toledo that night and when they crossed the state line over into Michigan their car died. Unlike mine it never restarted.

They said that they had tried and tried unsuccessfully to get it started. Mike said that nobody stopped and they began to get real worried, and real cold, as the night grew on. Brother Mike said that out in that open area of the freeway it didn't take long for them to start to feel the cold and wind. With no blankets and unsure where to walk they said they did not know what they were going to do.

They lived near Woodhaven, Michigan, so they were not familiar with the area so they did not consider attempting to leave the shelter of their car. As the time passed they were getting really cold and running out of options. They had no cell phone and when their options ran out they turned to the Lord for help. Brother Mike said just before I pulled up he said that he and his wife entered the throne room of prayer and began to pray. He said as they prayed they asked the Lord to send someone to help them in their time of need. He said we literally had just finished our prayer and Mike said he looked up and saw my car pull over.

As we sat there along the freeway we began to thank the God of Abraham, Isaac, and Jacob for His love and Mercy. As they warmed themselves I just relished the thought of how good that God is.

I checked my mirror and with no cars coming I pulled onto North bound I-75 and headed for Woodhaven. As we traveled I told them of my experience of just getting to school and back north to them. Brother Mike just cried. Not tears of sadness but tears of joy! He was just thanking me for obeying the spirit of God because he said he didn't know what would have happened to them if I would have just gone home. He told me that if I wanted to that I could just take them to the Pilot Center at I-75 at Nadeau Road in

Monroe and then he would have his daughter come and get them. It seemed like just a few minutes and we were there.

We went inside and I told them that it was an honor to help them. Again he cried as he and his wife gave me a hug and said goodbye. When I left the Pilot I began to thank God again for what He had done. From that night until the day we sold that Omni....it never stalled out again!

My Left Shoulder

It was late that night as the dispatcher said that live power lines had fallen on top of the house and were arching. The roof of that house happened to be metal thus creating an awesome light show when it arched. We responded with an engine company. As we prepared to formulate a plan I hyper extended my left arm and felt a sharp pain in my left shoulder, I couldn't even lift my arm up to touch my nose with my finger. I went to the ER to have the doctor check me.

After the ER visit I was sent the next day to see our Occupational Health Services doctor. He ordered several weeks of rest and then physical therapy. It was back to the OHS doctor and an order for two more weeks of PT. My arm was getting stronger but I did not have full range of motion with my arm so the rest and PT continued. Yet another visit to the OHS doctor and the decision was made to do an MRI of my shoulder.

The MRI showed that I had a full thickness tear of the Supraspinatus Muscle in my left rotator cuff. That even sounds like it hurts. Our OHS doctor decided to send me to an Orthopedic Surgeon. At my appointment the orthopedic doctor continued my PT hoping my arm would release. It felt like there was a "catch" in my left shoulder. With my arm out to my side I could only bring it up about 2/3 of the way. After this height it would stop and would not go any higher. With PT the pain was getter lesser and my ability to move it was better. I went back to the orthopedic doctor after about two weeks and he told me if it didn't release I would need surgery.

I have heard many horror stories about people having rotator cuff surgery. One guy in my PT group had 4 surgeries and he was still in PT and had not worked in years. I did not want this. A few days before I was scheduled to see the surgeon and begin to prep for surgery I sought God for His help. I earnestly prayed for God to release my shoulder and to heal me. I prayed about my fears and my concerns about being possibly disabled and not able to work. That night I fell asleep with a shoulder that was all messed up and when I woke up in the morning it had released.

I went to the orthopedic doctor and he couldn't believe it. He spent time manipulating my arm around it was not making any crackling and rubbing noises. After he reviewed my case he said there was no reason why I could not return to work with no restrictions.

Luis Santiago Uribe

Luis is my adopted son and he joined the Army after high school. He went to Basic Training and from there to Special Forces school. I went down to Fort Benning for his graduation ceremony. It was really nice to see him graduate from Special OPS school but it was sad too because I knew it wouldn't be long until he would be sent to Iraq. True to my fears we received word that his unit was being sent to Iraq.

He told me that the first night in Iraq that the Hummer that he was riding in got blown right out from under his team. It wasn't long after that that he took a bullet in the ceramic plate that fits inside his chest body armor. He told me how absolutely scared that he was during this whole ordeal. He said that it was definitely not like watching a war movie or playing a war video game. Each time that I went to church I requested prayer for him because I did not want him to get hurt or die.

On one particular mission Luis and his team were clearing a building. As they gathered near the front of the building they realized that one of their members was not with them. Being the leader he gave orders to the rest of the team to sit tight and that he would go back to find the soldier. Right after he left that area the building was hit by mortar fire and the mortars hit right where he would have been standing. He told me had it not been for that other soldier getting lost near the rear of the building he would have surely been hit and possibly killed during that mission that night. It is truly good to know that we have a God that hears our prayers when we pray and that our prayers can be answered on the other side of the globe!

Where We'll Never Grow Old

Albert Simpson was born and raised in Portsmouth, Ohio. He was a World War II veteran and after the war he was a partner in the family business called Simpson Steel Works. He and his wife, Margaret Louise Simpson had a daughter named Priscilla. Grandpa Simpson and Granny Simpson lived on Linden Street in Portsmouth, Ohio, until Grandpa got sick. Their daughter then had them moved to Ypsilanti so that she could better care for them. Grandpa was diagnosed with cancer and soon was placed in care of Hospice.

We lived south of Ypsilanti in Monroe at the time and we traveled up to see grandpa every chance that we could. While their mother was at work and the other boys were in school, my youngest son Mark and I would go up and sit with granny. Granny would mostly sit with grandpa and it was very hard for her not to cry. These two were a dictionary definition of what a married couple should be. She seldom ever left his side.

On this trip Mark and I left Monroe and as we were leaving Monroe I told Mark that when we get there that we should sing a song for granny. Since grandpa would sleep most of the time I wanted to dedicate more time helping granny. So as Mark and I turned onto I-275 off of Telegraph

Road I told him that we should sing "***Where We'll Never Grow Old***" for granny and he agreed. Page 296 in the familiar red Church Hymnal is where you will find this old time beloved song about heaven.

As we got onto the freeway we sang that song over and over again. Forward and then backward and all over again is how we sung it. God's spirit filled that little car as we sang as if we were singing it at Madison Square Gardens. We got off in Ypsilanti and in just a few minutes we were at the condo. As we walked into the apartment grandpa was in the hospital bed sleeping. Granny, true to her calling, was sitting next to his side. As her silent vigil was broken she greeted us with a big hug and a kiss. Mark was elated.

We sat and talked for a little while as granny told us about grandpa and his condition. As I sat there Mark came up and sat on my lap. I looked at him and I asked him if he was ready and he eagerly said yes. In a low and solemn tone we began to sing ***"Where We'll Never Grow Old."*** Like a shroud the spirit of the Lord came down around in that room and covered us. I don't know if I have ever felt the spirit of God come so greatly in my life. We sat there fighting back the tears as we sang all three verses of that song.

Granny with her head bowed just cried and cried. After the song was over we sat there as granny continued to cry and Mark got up and went over and sat on her lap. Through the tears she told us how much that it meant for us to come and visit and most of all sing for her. As we tried to tell her thank you she interrupted me and told us that we didn't really understand why that it meant so much. She went on to tell us that her mother never really sang that much but when she did her favorite song of all time was **_"Where We'll Never Grow Old!"_**

Mark and I were overjoyed as we left that day. I told Mark that as we neared that freeway going up to Ypsilanti that I knew in my heart that God wanted us to sing that song. I just didn't know why until granny told us why. It's good to know that when someone is in need of a blessing that God knows exactly what to do.

The Gas Gauge

My mom has never really driven a car. She tried one time to learn and after careening off of a telephone pole she gave up. Over the years we have joyfully been her taxi driver. When her and my Aunt Esther decided to go to Tennessee for one of their usual jaunts it was me that would take her to meet up with my aunt. This time it would be at my cousin Reda's house on Doty Road in the western part of Monroe County. As I went to bed my last thought before going to sleep was that I had just enough gas "fumes" to get me to the fire station. I thought "Oh well, tomorrow is tomorrow!"

If you ask anyone in my family they will tell you that I seldom put more than 5 or 10 dollars in my tank. Even on a long trip I will seldom put more than 20 dollars at a time. Don't know why it's just one of those quirky things that I do. I got up in the morning and as I packed my mom's stuff in my car I was reminded that I was already on fumes. I did the math and it is about 10 miles to Reda's and then 10 miles back to where I live. From our house it is another 5 miles to my fire station in the other direction.

As we got in the car I was about to tell my mom that I needed two things. First, I need gas money, and second I needed to go get gas before we were walking. As I started to break that news to her about needing gas for the trip God said, "Just drive!" Without saying one word to her I just pulled away from the house and headed for Reda's. Without making it obvious I looked at my gas gauge and the red line showed that I was now below empty. This meant that I was truly empty and literally on fumes!

Without a thought of my gas deficiency mom and I just talked and talked about her trip and all the things that they had planned. She had no idea that we were very close to walking. As we pulled into Reda's driveway I looked and the gas gauge marker was now totally to the "right" of the empty marker. I don't even want to imagine how I got that far except it be for the Lord! I loaded her stuff into my Aunt Esther's van and as they got ready to leave I told them that we needed to pray that God would watch over them and to give them travel grace. As they sat in the van, and me outside the driver's door, we prayed. Very seldom do we ever leave on the road that we fail to ask the Lord to watch over us and our trip. And they drove out of sight!

As I watched them drive out of my sight I turned around and just stood there laughing! My first thought was that "I" needed prayer because there probably was not enough gas to get me to the end of Reda's driveway.

As I stood there I tried to think of a game plan. I even turned to look around to see if I could find a gas can to put some gas in my car. As I started to think about what I would do the Lord just told me again, "Just drive!" Without much resistance I got in my car fired it up and headed to the fire station.

It was foggy that morning but in patches only. As soon as I made it down to Bluebush Road I was socked in and could only go about 10 miles per hour. I apologized to God because I had to laugh to keep from crying! How was I going to coast to work at 10 miles per hour? So I headed east on Bluebush and I thought that I would look down at the gas gauge to see how much further I was beyond empty and the gas gauge showed that I was actually "above" empty. Well, hallelujah!

As I drove I couldn't keep my eyes on the road because I kept watching the gas gauge. As I got closer to Sumpter Road the sun broke through the fog and fully illuminated a very large tree as I drove right for it. The sun glistened like a million lights as this tree was the only thing that I could see silhouetted through the fog. What looked like a million rays of sunlight burst around the limbs and branches of that tree. It was truly an awesome spectacle! I had never seen anything like that before. In shear wonder I gazed at that tree and knew for surety that God would get me to work safely.

When I passed that tree the fog cleared just as abruptly as it came. The road was clear and when I looked down at my gas gauge it had moved up showing that I had more gas now than I did a few minutes ago. By the time I reached the fire station I had "over" a quarter of a tank of gas showing on the gauge. There is no way that this happened without Godly intervention. I drove two more days after that before I got gas again!

Doug

Going up north has been a long standing tradition in my family. Volumes of books could never justly describe the fun that we have had over the years. Many memories that are worth more than gold and silver have been carved into my memory. This trip that we made several years ago is one of the greatest because it was smothered with events that many would have considered a travelers nightmare. It is in these times that I look to the Lord to see what that He wants me to see. Often times it has been a chance for me to spread the good news of Jesus Christ. This story is truly one of my favorites.

My van was packed and we headed to our first stop 15 minutes north of Monroe in a small town called Dundee, Michigan. We fueled up and grabbed our usual snacks and goodies. As we get ready to jump onto US 23 to head north we always stop and have a moment of prayer to ask God to watch over us and to give us travel grace. We finished our prayer and off we were to Wellston, Michigan, about 4 hours away.

About 45 minutes later we were just north of Ann Arbor and my van started missing like it was running out of gas. I exited the freeway and thanked God that we were only a few miles from home. As I went to get back onto US 23

"Southbound" to head back home my van quit running. My first thought was to call a tow truck and get us pulled home. As we sat there God began to deal with me and He laid part of a Bible scripture on my heart. The words were, "Neglect not so great a salvation." I know that I have read that but I wanted to look it up anyway. I grabbed my Bible and found where those words are at in the Bible.

It's in the book of Hebrews in the New Testament Chapter 2 and verse 3. It reads like this, "How shall we escape, if we neglect so great salvation; which at first began to be spoken by the Lord, and was confirmed unto us by them that heard him; God also bearing them witness, both with signs and wonders, and with divers miracles, and gifts of the Holy Ghost, according to his own will?" I read it over and over again trying to see what God was trying to show me. I then thought to myself, "Well Lord, what am I neglecting?"

I began to wonder if the Lord was trying to show me that I was neglecting His salvation, but I know that I had been saved and accepted Him into my life on February 11, 1990. I knew for a fact that was the day that I met Him and now know Him in a free pardon of sin.

I didn't really know what to do. I was literally sitting there not knowing which direction to take. I tried to start my van and it started and was running fine. As I pulled off the shoulder back onto the road I was faced with two options. If I went to the right I would be back on Northbound US 23 heading to our camp up north. If I went left I would be on the entrance ramp to Southbound US 23 heading home. God said to go north!

My kids are so used to these types of events and occurrences in my life that they seldom wonder about the outcome. I always tell them that God will make a way somehow. So, we are back heading north and our next stop is Birch Run.....maybe! About 35 miles from Birch Run my van started to miss and shake really bad. I pulled over and we sat there with it still running. I tried to pull back out onto the freeway and it stalled. The kids were not really worried as they just sat there talking. Immediately God brought that scripture back to my memory about neglecting His great plan of salvation.

After about 10 minutes I tried to start my van and again it fired right back up and was running fine. I pulled back onto the freeway and we were once again underway. I told the kids that we were going to step out of our normal routine and not stop at Birch Run. It seemed that my van was running for about 45 minutes and then it would stop. They agreed and away we went. As God would have it we were on that leg of the trip just shy of an hour and it started to shake and miss like it was running out of gas. We pulled over, sat and chatted, started it up again and we were on our way. For whatever reason this is how the trip was set to be.

As I came around the corner of Prunski and Dorothy Roads I saw my brother's place and thought to myself we were home free....kinda. As I pulled in front of the garage I reached up to shut the key off and my van moaned out like a blue whale getting run over by a semi truck and it shook and died! This time it didn't start back up. As is usual when we travel we gave the God of Abraham, Isaac, Jacob all the credit and thanks for getting us up north. We were going to be there for about 6 days so I said we can worry about the van later. We unpacked and settled in for a week of camping and hunting.

I knew that my van would be requiring some TLC so I went out to start it after a few days and it started. I decided to call the local grocery store/hardware/convenience store near our place for help finding a garage. I talked with Tom and he told me of a retired Navy man who lived behind the store that liked to tinker around on cars. He told me his name was Doug. I decided to give Doug a call to see if he could help me.

Doug told me that if it started to just drive it to his place behind the store. I headed that way for the 7 mile trip. As the store came into view my van started to run bad so I managed to just pull it into one of the parking spots at the store. It died and wouldn't start. Doug told me to just sit tight and that he would come over and pull me to his place. It seems, for whatever reason, that I get to sit along the roadside a lot. Soon I saw him driving around the lot looking for me. He towed me to his place and the search for a cure began.

Doug was not very tall and he was slender in build. He had a quiet demeanor about him and didn't speak a lot. He moved about with a graceful stride. His face was wrinkled and care worn and when I shook his hand I could tell he was a mechanic. His hands were clean but they were stained with grease and a multitude of healing cuts and scrapes so indicative of his years of working with his hands. He pulled my van inside his garage and went to work.

He soon told me that he thought that it was my fuel pump so it was off to the parts store to get a new one. After putting the new one on my van ran but not very well.

After trying other things it appeared as if nothing was going to resurrect my dead van. After hours of trying I think Doug realized that it was not going to work. He said that I may want to take it to another facility about 5 miles away so they could put it on the scope to do more checks.

I called Tom back at the store and told him Doug would not let me pay him. Tom said buy him a 12 pack of beer and call it quits. I told Tom that I did not know about that because I really don't like to buy beer for people. As I rode with Doug, as he pulled my van to the other shop, God brought back that scripture to me about neglecting His plan of salvation. As we drove to the garage across the way I realized that God allowed all of this to happen so I could tell Doug about the Lord and that God wanted me to tell Doug not to forsake His love and salvation.

After we dropped off my van at the other shop I tried to pay Doug and he wouldn't let me. I had to secure my van with the new shop owner so I did not get to talk with Doug that much before he left to go home. I had made arrangements for a ride back home to Monroe but I was determined to stop by Doug's house on the way to tell him about this whole ordeal and how that God did not want "him" to neglect God and His love and mercy. The next morning I got bad news from the shop. They said that my van was dead and probably worth no more than scrap! I inquired about a local scrap yard and there were none. The shop owner said he would give me five hundred for it.

We sat around the campsite that morning waiting for our ride to get there. I told my oldest son Mitchell that if my van was not fixable that I would need him to come and get us. I made that call and he was on his way. After Mitchell arrived we quickly packed up his car and prepared to head home. I told everybody that I needed to go and see Doug one more time before we headed home. I knew in my heart that everything that had happened from the time we left Monroe until this very moment was orchestrated by God so that I could tell Doug the good news about Jesus Christ and how that He loved him. As we made our way back to Doug's place it was about 6pm and he was not home. My heart was broken!

I waited around for a bit hoping he would come home but he didn't. Knowing we had about a four hour drive ahead of us we set out for home. It was now past 6pm and I told everybody that I would see Doug the next time that we came up. I watched intently as his home faded from my view. All the way home I couldn't help but think how that this whole trip was for one purpose and one purpose only and that was for me tell a man that I had never met before about Christ.

It's funny how that God works! Not Ha Ha but interesting. Since I left Monroe with a Mercury Villager van and came home riding on somebody else's dime I knew the story would be one noteworthy to tell. Since everybody I knew would ask me about this excursion it would give me another chance to tell how that God works and how that He loves us. After telling the experience about a hundred times I noticed one interesting staple every time I told the story. Each hearer of the story would eventually get around to asking me something like this, "So, you're not ticked off that your van died and you had all that trouble?" I would simply smile and ask, "What trouble?"

I was asked many times as to what I was going to do for a car. My answer, "God will surely make a way!" I have been able to share this story with countless people and I am amazed at how many said that they would have been mad or upset if this happened to them. I was worried a few times but not scared or mad. God showed me why that all of these events took place. It was an opportunity for me to share the good news of Jesus Christ.

I was saddened that I did not get to see Doug before I left to come home. I began to seek God as to what that I should do. God laid it on my heart to buy him a Bible and send it to him. As soon as I got home I did just that. I bought him a beautiful leather bound King James Version Bible and had his name put on it in gold letters. I wrote down the whole story how that we began a trip, almost didn't make it, and how that God was the author of it all.

I don't know if Doug received that Bible or not. I put twenty dollars in the card that I sent and a marker where the verse was that I used. Hebrews is one of the richest books in the Bible and often times I feel that in some ways we may all neglect this great salvation plan that God sent down to man. For me to go through all that I did and to lose my mode of transportation in the process just to tell another man not to turn God away was truly worth it! To God be the glory!

Uncle Herbert

As I drove down the road one day I just kept humming a few words to a Gospel song. It was only a few words of the song but it was powerful in the Spirit of God. For the life of me I could only remember these words, "And I know I know he holds the future." This went on for weeks and I could only remember those few words. I asked my mom one day if she knew the song that I was trying to remember and she said no. So that's the way it was for several weeks.

As I was losing my mind over this song I went back to my mom and asked her if she had thought of it and she told me no. She then told me to get in touch with Tom Treece to see if he could help me. In our little town of Monroe, Michigan, Tom Treece is a hero to many. He is a devout Christian who proudly proclaims the goodness of God and His son Jesus. Mr. Treece is an accomplished musician and has a lengthy background in the knowledge of Gospel hymns. I called Tom and he giggled and told me that was an easy one for him. He said, "Those words are from the song by Bill and Gloria Gaither called "Because He Lives."

As soon as those words came out of his mouth I remembered! I asked Tom if by chance he had the words to that song written down and he told me no. I was now off to our local music store in search of those words. As I drove to the mall I began to ask God as to why He was burdening my heart so heavy about this song. My answer did not come! When I got to the mall I went to the Gospel song area and started looking through about 200 CD's. After quite some time I found a CD that contained the words to this song. It was the last CD in the area.

I was now excited to hear the entire song so I went home and must have played that song over and over again about 20 times. I then sat down and copied the words onto paper. I got my guitar out and then found the key that I was comfortable with and I began to sing that song. I sang it 20 times.

While I sat there listening to it over and over again and then playing it over and over again I couldn't help but wonder why I was doing this. Again, I set out to seek God about it in prayer. Again, I received no word from heaven! For the next few weeks this song kept reverberating in my heart, mind, and soul relentlessly. Each time I sang it, hummed it, thought about it, meditated on it God just blessed me beyond measure. I then knew for a fact that God was doing this for a reason I just didn't know what as of yet. As with all of the other wonderful times like this I knew He would show me.

I was driving down the road one afternoon and the Lord really began to deal with me about this song and I just gloried in the blessing that He was giving me. Without asking Him this time God spoke to my heart and said, "I want you to sing this for Herbert!" He showed me that He wanted me to travel nearly 500 miles to see my Uncle Herbert and to sing this song for him. God never said why, He just said go! I went home put the words to that song in my guitar case and prepared to travel to Tennessee.

A group of us headed south and while there my plan was to go and to see my Uncle Herbert and to tell him all that God had showed me over many weeks of preparing me for the trip. We traveled first to New Tazewell, Tennessee, and stayed there for several days. My plan was to see Herbert on my way home back to Michigan. While visiting with my family in New Tazewell we regularly would get out our musical instruments and sing and fellowship around the old home place. The old wrap around porch was an awesome place to sit and sing. This trip though would be different!

For whatever reason I never once got my guitar out of my van! I have never done that before. We would always travel around to different churches and would sing during their services. Again, for whatever reason, I still went to church but never touched my guitar. Several times I was asked by my family if I had brought my guitar and if so why was I not playing with them. Again, I didn't know at the time why that I was not playing but I found out later. God knew exactly what He was doing. I didn't know until the end of the matter.

The day came that we were leaving New Tazewell and as we prepared to leave my cousin Randy asked me if he could hitch a ride to Monroe with us. We were glad to help him get home. We loaded up and headed for Herbert's home town of Lafollette, Tennessee. The ride north to Herbert's house was only about a 45 minutes long. As we drove on the main road to make our way to Lafollette, the devil just kept telling me to go on our way to Monroe and to forget Herbert! The devil began to tell me that we had gotten a late start and that I could just sing for Herbert some other time. As we got closer to the turn off to Herbert's house the devil tried everything to stop me.

I have found over the years that when God wants me to do something that the devil is also present to try and stop or hinder me from obeying God's word. As we got to the turn off I just headed west to Herbert's house. Six miles later and I could see my Uncle Herbert's and my Aunt Esther's house. I was really nervous as I pulled in only to find out that he was not home. My heart was broken to say the least. I went to my Aunt Elsie's house right next door and they told me that he may be at his daughter Sue's house.

As I pulled into the driveway Sue came out. She said that her dad was in the house visiting. I asked her to go and get him because I wanted to do something for him. Minutes later he appeared from around the house. After a few hugs were given I had a captive audience. There were about 10 of us standing around in a small group as I told my story of the things that God had placed on my heart with regard to that song, "Because He Lives." I told them all about how the Lord had done all of these things so that I could come and sing this for him. I told about how I did not even touch my guitar the whole time that I was down in Tennessee. With tears in my eyes I asked him if I could sing that song for him. He told me yes by all means.

I went over to the back of my van and got my guitar out and opened the case only to find that the words were missing. I "thought" that I had put them in my case before I left but I didn't. I knew right then why that I had not gotten my guitar out while on my trip. No matter how many times I sing a song I almost invariably have to read the words as I sing. That may sound weird but that is just the way that I am! My heart sank into my shoes but I knew that I did not want to leave without singing that song.

Nobody could see me because I was behind my van. I began to cry because I didn't know what to do. Once again, the Lord came on the scene and said, "It will be alright go and sing!" Just as God revealed that to me all of my fears and anxieties were lifted from me. I walked back over to the group that had gathered in the driveway and prepared to sing. Just before I sang there appeared a large cone of glistening light that settled down over all of us. Everybody standing there saw as it came down like a large dome and covered us. I had never seen anything like that before in my life. It was an awesome sight to behold.

As we stood under that dome I sang, "Because He Lives" for my Uncle Herbert and the mighty Spirit and power of God just flooded our souls. The sound of that song just resonated inside that dome and I never missed a word. When finished I looked around and not a dry eye could be seen. That dome of light went back up just like it came down.

We all hugged again and we said our goodbyes and we headed back toward the main road that would lead us home to Michigan. From Lafollette we went through Harrogate and then on to Middlesboro, Kentucky. As we neared the north end of Middlesboro the road begins a gradual incline. As I got to that hill I noticed that my van would not go any faster. I gave the van more gas but all we did was slowed down. No matter how much gas I gave it we were slowing down. The engine was running fine. My first thought was that we lost our transmission.

My cousin Randy asked me what the problem was and I told him that we did not pray for travel grace. We seldom ever travel that we don't have special prayer that God would watch over us and keep us safe. Inside the van was my three sons Mitchell, Matthew, and Mark. Randy and I sat up front. I looked at all of them and quickly said, "Guys! We forgot to pray and to ask the Lord to watch over us and to give us travel grace. Right then, as we slowed to about 20 miles an hour, we began to really pray for God to help us. As we prayed I noticed that my van started going faster. By the time we finished our prayer we were going 55 miles per hour. I didn't have a clue what happened but we were on our way again.

We arrived safely in Monroe at around one in the morning. I dropped off Randy at home and the boys and I headed home. The next morning I thought that I should probably take my van and get it checked. I "drove" my van to the transmission shop and asked the service tech if he could check it out for me. He assured me that they would give it a once over. When it was my turn I "drove" my van into the garage bay so the mechanic could put it on the lift and check it out. I then went to the customer waiting area.

About 45 minutes later the service tech asked me if I had paid the tow truck driver or not. I told him that I was not sure what he meant. He said that it is customary that the tow bill could be paid by the garage and then just added to my bill. A told him that I did not have a tow bill. He then asked me who towed my van to the shop. I told him that I drove it there. He just laughed and said, "No you didn't!" I assured him that I did drive it there and that I also drove it into the garage bay. He smiled at me and looked around at the others there and said, "There is no way you drove this van here!" I again told him that I did.

He said, "Wait here!" As I stood there waiting I was wondering if I had lost my mind because I know for a fact that I drove my van there that morning. After a few minutes the man came back to the desk and asked me to come back and to talk to the mechanic. As I walked back to my van there were several people standing around. The mechanic asked about the tow.

I told him that I drove my van there that morning and never had it towed. He had his hands cupped together and as he opened them there were about six to eight pieces of metal covered with transmission oil. He said that when he pulled the transmission oil pan off that all of those pieces of metal and more were in the pan. He said, "Sir, you did not have a working transmission." I then began to tell them the story of what started out as a few words contained in a song that turned into a trip to Tennessee to sing for an Uncle and how that God had richly blessed me beyond measure.

As I told them more of the story they just marveled at me. I told them how that a dome of protection came down from out of the sky to protect me as I sang for my Uncle Herbert. I also told them how that when the van quit running that prayer changed things and that I believe that God brought us all the way home without a working transmission! As they stood there listening to me another mechanic from back in the garage came up and said that he believed that God had done all of this.

To this day I am not sure why that God wanted me to sing that particular song for Uncle Herbert. All I do know is that it was one of the greatest experiences that I have ever had in my life. Endless miracles!!!

Tornadoes on Norway

Growing up in the subdivision called Evergreen Acres has been a highlight of my youthful years. It is a dead end subdivision made up of six streets and two main entrance streets. We lived on the last street in the sub on Norway drive. As a kid growing up we used to play and hunt in the large field behind our house. Unfortunately now it is a trailer park. We enjoyed the Michigan weather of four seasons. Spring, summer, fall and winter each had their own particular characteristics that made them special. The only one that I did not like was springtime due to the tornado alarms.

It would seem like an ordinary day and then the sounds of the neighborhood would be deafened by the sound of the tornado siren. We knew that this was a real threat so we took them very seriously. Our house was one of the few that had a basement so when the siren would go off it wouldn't be long before our basement would have guests. I had visions of this massive tornado coming right for our house and would try to run. As I struggled to get away I would scream and then wake up realizing it was only a dream.

I was too young to understand all of the meteorological mumbo jumbo, so without even knowing how, I depended on a small group of people who really believed in the power of prayer.

I remember the warning that would come across the TV screen telling us that we should take cover in a basement or crawl space. We would scurry down the stairs and go up against the wall that faced the west. We were told that if the tornado hit that wall that it would carry the house off of the foundation and we would hopefully not get hit with any debris. I remember many times as I would huddle with my brothers and sisters up against that wall. I remember these events as if they happened yesterday.

Another thing that I vividly remember was my Uncle Lloyd and Aunt Mary Lee coming down to be with us. My mom, Aunt Mary Lee, and Uncle Lloyd would tell us to take shelter in the area at the base of the wall. They, in turn, would take shelter in the power of prayer! I would listen intently as they would ask God to spare us and our neighborhood homes. They would be praying that God would let the tornado pass right by us or go over us. Many times I heard as if it were a train buzzing over our house only to find out later that the storm did no damage or harm to us. It seemed odd too that our basement would be full of neighbors but not all believed that God was able to protect us.

One of my Aunt Mary Lee's favorite statements was to ask God to do something and then she would give her trademark statement, "And God I ask this in the name of Jesus Christ of Nazareth!" She knew that she could trust the Lord and she was not shy about it. The sky would darken and soon I would see her coming down the road with her handkerchief in her hand and my Uncle Lloyd in tow. As soon as she would get into the basement she would make the call and say that it was time to pray.

From the time I was a kid up to and including the present day, I don't ever remember a tornado hitting our subdivision. I believe that the years of praying and seeking God to watch over us really made a difference. I remember as some would make fun of those that prayed, but the prayer warriors didn't mind. They knew in whom they believed in and the blessings of God are worth searching for.

Back Up

I worked in the City of Taylor as a Paramedic for a private ambulance company. My partner at the time was Jim Polgar. Jim was a resident of the City of Taylor and during our shift we would routinely go to his home, Many times we would go there to hang out with his mom and sister or better yet we would see what kind of food we could scavenge. Since we worked 24 hour shifts we would stop by his house because that many hours at one time meant three full meals and several snack times in between.

In this story of God's love we start out at his house during a normal shift. It was about 4 o'clock in the afternoon on a warm summer day. When we walked out to the ambulance Jim jumped into the driver's side and I got into the passenger side. This driving arrangement would be a significant detail in this event. As Jim backed down his driveway we looked out of the driver's side window and several doors down three kids were playing in the front yard. As Jim continued to back down the driveway the kids all grabbed their chest as if they were having a heart attack and they all three fell to the ground. As was usual when we saw kids do this we got a good laugh out of it and we would hit the siren. We see kids do this all the time.

We sat there just for a second as the kids lay on the ground. Again we laughed and Jim pulled out onto his street to head south. This direction of travel would be going away from where the kids were. As he accelerated to about ten miles per hour a weird feeling came over me. I sensed danger and I told him to, "Back up!" Jim looked at me and laughed and asked, "What!" I looked at him with a very serious face and said, "We have to back up!" He again asked me why and I told him that something was dreadfully wrong.

We were now about ten houses away from where the kids were and we were just barely rolling. From my vantage point I could not see anything behind me on the side of the street where the kids were playing. There were no windows and from where I was sitting I could not see anything in the mirrors on the ambulance. Jim looked at me puzzled and asked, "Back up where?" I said, "Hurry up and back up to where those kids are in that front yard!" He then asked me, "Are you crazy or what?" I told him no but I knew something was really wrong.

Reluctantly he put the ambulance into reverse and slowly backed up to a position right in front of the house where the kids had been playing. Without any doubt that something was wrong I bolted out the passenger side of that ambulance and ran towards that house and there I saw her!

As I came around the back of the ambulance I saw the seven year old boy and the six year old girl looking down on the porch at the eight year old girl who was lying there motionless. My heart sank as I ran even faster to get to her. She was not moving and she was not breathing. I knew I had to do something and do it quick!

As we backed down Jim's driveway those three kids all gasped and moaned as if to be having a heart attack and then fell onto the ground. As we pulled away we saw that all three had stood up and were running around. At that time nothing seemed out of the ordinary. As we drove away what we didn't know was that when the oldest girl gasped and grabbed her chest she sucked a piece of hard candy into her upper airway.

As the other two kids were just running in circles and laughing she ran towards the porch so that she could get to the house to find help. It didn't take long in her moment of panic to go down. As she lay there on the porch the other kids talked to her thinking she was just playing. She was just minutes away from death. As I got to her lifeless body I lifted her up and laid her over my leg. With one knee on the ground and her lying face down on my other leg I held her face up and with the other hand I delivered a forceful blow to the middle of her back. It only took one hit and the foreign body that had completely occluded her airway popped out onto the ground. She immediately took one long deep breath.

From the time we stopped until I had her airway cleared could not have taken more than thirty seconds. Jim was still in the driver's seat. When he saw me clear her airway he came flying out of his seat to see what was going on. The girl was now breathing normally and her mom was with her. We told her mom that we strongly recommend that she go to the hospital to be checked and mom agreed. We loaded her onto the stretcher and headed for Heritage Hospital. By the time we arrived a few minutes later she seemed to be doing just fine.

After we took her back for the doctor to check her Jim asked me one compelling question, "How did you know?" I told him that I just had the weirdest feeling come over me that something was really wrong. Jim again pointed out that from where I was in the passenger seat that it was impossible for me to make any visible observation of what those kids were doing. While still at the ER, Dr. Muraba came up to me and said that the girl would probably have died right there on her porch if we would not have backed up. He said that he would probably release her after some observation and a few tests.

His Name was Collins

I had gotten off work that morning from my 24 hour shift and "my plans" were to get my check and to be on the road headed to New Tazewell, Tennessee. My wife and boys were already there and my plans were to be there in time for supper. It's amazing how motivating soup beans and cornbread can be if it means eating them in Tennessee! As I just said, "My plans" were to go and get my check and then head south. Unfortunately, my plans don't always equal up to "God's plans!" And now all of the obstacles!

They told us at work that a problem in accounting caused a situation whereby our checks would not be available until later in the afternoon. Bother! I decided that since I did not have enough money to head out yet that I would get my oil changed. I got there and I think everybody in Monroe was in line at this particular shop to get their oil changed. I was steaming just a bit. After the oil change I got something to eat.

As afternoon came upon me I called about my paycheck and they said "maybe" in a few hours we would get them! Seriously! It is now approaching 4 o'clock and no check. I called work again and they said "possibly" between 4 and 5 we might get them. I really wanted to get on the road and couldn't understand all of the delays. I called Brother Delmar. He told me to come and see him.

Reverend Delmar Moore is the Pastor of Grace Missionary Baptist Church. He lives over by my fire station and I have always been able to depend on him if I needed help. I got there and started my lengthy story of all of the delays and kept using the word, "unfortunately" during my ranting. As is his typical routine he would just laugh at all of my anguish. He then said that God's plans are the only ones that really matter. He said that there was surely a reason why I did not get my check. He said that the Lord did not want me to leave this morning and I am confident that He is going to show you why. Just be patient and let God do His perfect work. I knew Brother Delmar was right but I wanted to leave earlier that day.

Brother Delmar gave me money to head south and we had prayer before I left his house. I went to the gas station and filled my tank and headed for southbound I-75. As I turned my car to get onto the entrance ramp I noticed way down where the ramp meets the freeway that a young man was standing there obviously looking for a ride.

As tears filled my eyes God told me to pick him up. I knew right then why that I had been delayed so much. It was now nearly 6 o'clock and I was just getting on the freeway.

He was tall and had red hair. He was wearing a green military coat. As I pulled up I saw that his nametag on the coat said, "Collins." I pulled over and asked him where he was headed and he said, "New Tazewell, Tennessee!" Now I was really fighting back the tears as I told him to get in because that is where I was headed. He opened up the back door and put his green Army duffle bag in the back seat and jumped in. He shook my hand, said his name was Collins, and we were on our way.

I was reeling with joy because I knew that God has now showed me why that I had so many "unfortunate" delays throughout the day. For this young soldier, however, it was needful and actually "fortunate" for him that I was.

As we got underway he told me that he was on leave from the Army and that his family was from Monroe. He said that he had been visiting with family but really wanted to go to New Tazewell because that is where that his mom lived. He said that he had not seen her in about a year. Not having enough money even for a bus ticket he decided to hitch hike to Tennessee in hopes of seeing her. On the outside I showed little signs of emotion but on the inside God was pouring out a blessing on me that I could hardly contain.

After only traveling about a half an hour I started wondering if he was hungry. Not wanting to embarrass him I told him that I was starving and that I wanted to go through a drive through and get some food. He looked down at the floor and said that he didn't have any money. I told him not to worry about it because I didn't have any money on me either. He looked at me with the most unusual look on his face. He then asked me as to how that we would get any food without money. As I smiled at him I said, "Trust me!"

We pulled into the drive through at the fast food place and ordered our food. I pulled around to the window and he watched intently as I paid for the food with cash. As we pulled back onto the freeway I realized that now was the time to tell him about my day. I told him about how that if anything could go wrong it did. I told him how that my check was delayed and I wondered how I could get money to go. I told him about every delay that I had and how frustrated that I was over the whole ordeal. He was still wondering about how I paid for the food. I told him that I did not have any money so I thought that I better explain. I told him that I had money and that it was borrowed from the Pastor from church and that we were both traveling on borrowed money.

I told him about Brother Delmar and how he told me that all of these things happened to me today for a reason. The reason was so that I could arrive at that entrance ramp just in time to take a young soldier to Tennessee so he could see his mother. Even more importantly it would be an opportunity for me to tell him about the Lord! Now that I had a captive audience I was able to share many of the stories of the road where my plans were not always God's plans.

As nightfall took us over we chatted about the goodness of the Lord. I knew for a fact that it was Godly intervention why my day was so messed up and how important it was that we ride south together. The Spirit of God was so great in my car as I shared the good news about Jesus and told how important it was that he be saved. Mr. Collins listened very intently as I shared my many testimonies about God and His love for us. My thoughts were not about my messed up day any more.

It seemed liked just minutes that we were on the road and soon a sign read Cincinnati 50 miles. I told him that we would be in Kentucky soon and then on to New Tazewell. He then told me that if I could take him to Florence

Kentucky that he would be just fine. He said that his sister lives in Florence and she told him if he was able to get there that he could spend the night with her and then the next morning that she would take him the rest of the way to see his mom. I told him that I would take him to the big truck stop in Florence with one condition. He asked, "What would that be?" I told him that at this truck stop that they serve a mean steak. I told him that we could get a steak and at least get a late supper in while waiting on his sister to get there. He said that it was getting late and that he was excited about seeing his sister.

As we got to the truck stop he called his sister and she said it would take her about 15 minutes to get there. My heart felt like it would burst. As we talked I was fully persuaded that this was exactly how God wanted my day to go. We shook hands and I wished him well. He waved as I drove on my way. For most of the rest of my drive I cried. In a way I was upset because I was so panicked over my delays earlier in the day. I knew, though, that a young military man was safe, would get to see his mom, and that he got to hear about the good news of Jesus Christ.

The Fever

My partner and I received a call to a large hospital in the western part of the city of Detroit. When we got there it was a stat Advanced Life Support inter-hospital transfer of a six year old boy with an uncontrollable fever. When we arrived the ER doctor was greatly concerned because nothing that they were doing was bringing the fever down. As the ER nurse gave me report she told me that the last rectal temperature was 106. She said we were taking the boy to Children's Hospital in downtown Detroit. We readied our equipment.

As we prepared to load him he appeared very sleepy. His skin was very warm to the touch. He didn't say anything as we loaded him onto the stretcher. We advised the mother that she could ride in the ambulance but would not be allowed to be in the patient compartment. My fear was that if he went into a seizure that I would have my hands full taking care of him. I explained my concerns to mom and she told me that she would be fine riding up front. She got into the front passenger seat of our unit and we left.

As I sat in the back of the ambulance with the boy I read the nurse's notes about his visit to the ER that day. Several attempts by the ER doctors and nurses proved futile. This fever was hanging on! As I sat there reading, the boy never took his eyes off of me. I asked him if he was ok and he didn't speak a word he just nodded his head yes. I put the nurse's notes down and I began to tell him about the Lord. I told him that in the Bible in the Book of James that it talks about people being sick and getting prayed for. As I talked to him his mom was listening.

We were about 10 minutes from Children's Hospital and I asked him if I could anoint him with oil and pray for him like it says to in St. James Chapter 5:14. I looked at mom and she was willing to try anything at this point to get this deadly fever down. I told him that I would pray that the Lord would touch him and to take this fever away. I told him that I believed that God would touch him. I then asked him if he believed that the Lord would touch and he nodded yes.

I took my bottle of anointing oil out of my duffle bag and put some on my fingers. I asked him if he was ready and he again nodded yes. I put my hand on his forehead and began to pray and to ask God to take away his fever in the name of Jesus. The prayer ended and I looked up and his mom never took her eyes off of him. Within about a minute or so we were at Children's Hospital.

We backed into the ER entrance and unloaded him and took him into the hospital. As we walked through the ER doors I felt his head and he was cold to the touch. The fever was gone. As we got to the nurses station the clerk asked if we were the transfer with the fever. I told her yes. She called to one of the nurses and told her that we had arrived. When the nurse came up to me for report I told her that he did not have a fever anymore. She then asked me if I had given him any meds enroute to Children's. I told her no and then she asked me what his temp was as we transferred him. I again told her that he did not have any fever at all. She gave me "that" look and went over to the boy and began to feel his head and arms. I told her that he was as cold as a cucumber.

The mom came over to where we were and I told her to feel him. He was cold and his temp was normal. He sat up and talked to her and I and he looked very different than he did at first. Within a few minutes one of the Pediatric doctors came over to me to ask me about the little boy. I told her that the last temp at the transferring hospital was 106 rectally. After we arrived to the receiving hospital it was normal. The doctor asked me if I had an explanation and I asked her if I could tell her the truth about the matter. She said, "Of course!" I told her that we prayed and that God touched him!

With a look of disdain she said, "What is his temp now?" I said, "Normal, go ahead and feel his head he is as cold as a cucumber!" With great reluctance she felt his head and then his arms. She sighed and told us to take him to a room and then she told the nurse to get another temp on him. As I wheeled him into the room the little boy just looked up at me and smiled. As mom filed in behind us I told her that God really moved in the back of that ambulance and that He touched her little boy. She agreed and gave me a hug and we were on our way to the next call.

The Wet Pillow

As I pointed out in another chapter Grandpa Simpson was sick with cancer. He was brought by me from Portsmouth Ohio to Ypsilanti by ambulance. He stayed with his daughter Priscilla in her condo on Ford Lake. As time drew near he was placed under the care of Hospice and the nurses made regular visits to see him. The nurses told us that he was really bad and that it would not be long until he would pass away. We were truly broken hearted.

After several weeks of Hospice I got the call that I was dreading. My wife called and said that the Hospice nurse was at the condo and that death was imminent. I knew that my wife was really upset and I told her that I was going to go into my prayer room at the fire station and to seek God on grandpa's behalf. I went upstairs and lay on my face before God to ask Him to have mercy on grandpa.

As I prayed I began to ask God to grant grandpa a chance to cry out to Him and to plead for mercy. All I kept thinking about during my prayer time was that grandpa needed to really cry out in this great time of need. In the Bible we read of many places where people cried out to God for mercy, healing, forgiveness, compassion, and loving kindness. Saints and sinners alike sought Jesus in their time of need and many did it by crying out to Him as He passed through their towns and cities.

In Psalms chapter 6 David is tired and weary and hurting. In verse 6 he says, "I am weary with my groaning; all the night make I my bed to swim; I water my couch with my tears." (KJV Psalms 6:6) I just kept thinking how that King David was at a low time in his life and he sought God with many tears. I must have prayed for about 45 minutes pleading with God to let grandpa cry out just one more time before it was too late. After I finished my prayer I went back downstairs to my bed and tried to go back to sleep.

It was about 1o'clock when I got to bed. As soon as I lay down I heard a knock at the door. I got up and went to the back of the station and looked out of the door and nobody was there. I then walked up to the front office area of the station to see if the person knocking was up there. Again, nobody was there. Each time I traversed the station bay floors I could still hear somebody knocking. No matter which door or window I looked out of nobody was there. I also noted that no cars or bicycles were in the driveway. I then walked around the inside area of the bay again haunted by the knocking but nobody was there. I decided that I would go back to bed.

Just as my head hit the pillow the phone rang. It was my wife and she told me that grandpa had just died. I told her that I would call in relief and that she should bring the boys and come and get me. When she got there we headed for Ypsilanti. The nurse said that she would leave him there for a bit so we could come to see him and to help granny. Not much was said on the trip up to Ypsilanti. My mind was racing with the thought about grandpa and if he tried to cry out on God. The door knocking thing also kept resounding in my ears. We made it to Ypsilanti and we went in to visit.

I waited as others went in to see him and then the nurse took me in. As he laid there I just couldn't stop thinking about him and if he took the time to cry out to God. Grandpa had not spoken to anyone and had been in a comatose state for a little while. That is why that I prayed the more earnest for his soul. As I looked down on the pillow it was soaked around the right and left side. By his ears and the sides of his face the pillow was really wet. I about shouted for joy. I said to the nurse, "Look at his pillow how wet it is!" She couldn't believe how wet that it was. She then looked at me and said, "He must have been sweating." I told her no way was that sweat.

She then took a closer look and said, "His pillow on the sides is soaked!" I told her that it was definitely not sweat. She then asked me what I thought it was and I said, "Tears!" She asked, "Tears?" I told her all about how that I was at work and the knocking sound and how that I had prayed that grandpa would cry out to God for his salvation. She said, "No I don't think its tears it's got to be sweat." I then told her, "Then let's take a look!"

I lifted up grandpas arms and felt in his arm pits and they were parched! I rolled him on his side and ran my hand down the middle of his back and he was dry as cotton. I then put my hand between his thighs and he was dry as a bone. I then rubbed his chest and not one drop of sweat was on his body. The nurse looked at me with an intriguing look and said he is completely dry except around his face and the pillow is soaked. She said, "I have no explanation for you!" I told her that I had one for her.

I prayed that God would allow him one more chance to cry out to Him for salvation so that he would not be lost for all eternity. There was no other explanation that anyone could give me as to why that pillow was soaked. I believe with everything in me that a miracle took place there that night. I thank the Lord for His love and mercy.

The Cell Phone

My wife's dad and step mom live in Vanceburg, Kentucky, just a short jaunt over the Ohio River near Portsmouth, Ohio. She had planned on her and the boys to make a trip down to visit. I was working at the fire station so I couldn't go. I asked her to stop and see me for hugs and kisses before they headed out for their trip. So around 5 that night she and the three sons stopped out to see me. After we chatted for a bit they started to load up in the car to leave.

Just as she was getting ready to get in the car, my partner Tom came over with this large nylon bag. He told my wife that she should take this large contraption with her. She asked, "What is it?" Tom said, "It's a cell phone!" I looked into the bag and it had a hand set with push dial phone characteristics and a cord that attached to the rest of this large bag. She handed it back to him and said, "No thanks." He handed it back and told her to take it. This went on for a few minutes until he convinced her to take it. So Tom took it out of the bag and showed her how to use it. She reluctantly took it and they were on their way.

Within a few hours they were at her dad's and were enjoying their stay. Her, the three boys, and a beagle puppy named "Yogi" would spend the next few days in Kentucky and then they would travel back home.

The trip is usually about 4 hours and is mostly on open highway. If she plans to skip the bypass route then she has to drive in downtown Columbus on a bad road numbered 315. There are no shoulders, high walls all around, and the neighborhood is a little less than desirable. On the way home she took 315 and the weather was very stormy. High winds and blinding rain is what she met in Columbus. Right in the very worst part of 315 her car stopped running. She was barely able to get it to the side of the road. She said that even when a small car drove by it shook her car violently.

The car was running but wouldn't move. She said that she had the wipers on full blast and still could not see out of the windshield. The car then stalled and they were helpless to move. The traffic was rush hour and she had no idea what to do. She then remembered that Tom had given her that overgrown bag with an old cell phone in it. She powered it up and dialed our home. I was home and when I answered it I could tell by her voice that she was scared and that their situation was precarious. She gave me their location and I told her that I would get on the phone and get help out to them as quickly as I could. Just then a car pulled in front of her.

By her voice I could tell that she was in a panic. I told my wife to try and stay calm but to no avail. I grabbed a piece of paper and told her to read me the license plate number and to give me a description of the car. Just then she said that it looked like a State of Ohio Government license plate. She said as the car backed up to her she thought that she could barely read that this was a State of Ohio Corrections Department vehicle. My fears started to lesson a bit.

I told my wife to stay on the phone and to not hang up. As the person got out of the State car my wife noticed that it was a woman. As the woman ran up to the driver's side window she told my wife that she was with the State of Ohio Corrections Bureau and that she would stay with them until help arrived. Our hearts were relieved. The lady was a high ranking official with the Ohio Department of Corrections and she called her husband to come and help my wife and kids.

Her husband arrived and he was a high ranking member of the US Post Office in Columbus. He tried to get the car to run to no avail. He had it towed to a dealership and they determined that it was the serpentine belt that had broken. It was now late and they could not fix it so the service rep at the dealership said that they would fix it in the morning. As my wife and boys and a beagle puppy sat there they didn't know what to do next. The lady and her husband told them they could come to their home and wait there until I could get there.

When my wife got to their house she called me and told me where they were. She told me that the man and woman were going to let them stay with them until I could get down there. I told her that I was in the process of getting a car to drive. We only had one car so I had to borrow wheels to go and get them. My sister Melissa worked back then at the Bob Evans restaurant at I-75 and North Dixie Highway. She told me that I could take her car.

When I got to the Bob Evans it was about 7pm and there were storms all up and down I-75 all the way through to

Kentucky. Public Safety officials were warning people not to travel unless absolutely necessary. Rain, hail, tornadoes, high winds, and flooding were wreaking havoc on motorists. I didn't feel that I had much choice in the matter. My wife and kids were staying with a family that they had never met. I knew only one thing to do; I called my Aunt Mary Lee for prayer!

I told her all that had happened and that I was afraid to travel alone in that storm. She told me that we would pray and that God would go with me and that I did not have to fear and that I would not be alone during the trip.

As I stood there in the vestibule of that Bob Evans, Aunt Mary Lee and I earnestly prayed that the Lord would go with me and to protect me. Aunt Mary Lee said that God would go before me and that He would show me a sign that He was with me and that I would be ok. She finished that prayer in her trademark fashion by saying, "And God I thank you in the name of Jesus Christ of Nazareth!" Amen and Amen. I thanked her for praying with me and I went out to my sister's car and headed south.

When I turned to get on the entrance ramp to southbound I-75 I noticed that the storm was just as bad as they said it was....with one exception! There was an opening above my car and the light of the moon was shinning brightly through that opening. It was pouring rain on the northbound side of I-75 and not one drop of water was hitting my windshield. I never once turned my wipers on all the way to Columbus although I could see it raining all around me. In the headlights of the oncoming cars in the northbound side I could see the rain whipping and blowing.

Out of Findley, Ohio, I took the connector to US 23 to head to Columbus. Just north of Columbus there is a Cattleman's Dairy Store and that is where I met with the man who had tried to get my car started. After talking for a minute he told me to follow him to their home. As I drove I just wanted to cry! These people were going out of their way to help us and they didn't even know us. As we entered this very upscale neighborhood I marveled at the great homes with their lavish surroundings. As we pulled up in front of his house I was captured in awe by its size and beauty.

I pulled into the driveway behind him and he pulled into the garage and shut the door. I got out and walked up to the front door. As I stood there I began to knock on the front door and a sign that was posted on the middle of the front door caught my eye. It read, "The Holy Spirit of God is welcome in our Home!" Now I knew why that they stopped to help. They were Christians! Again I wanted to cry. As I stood there the door opened up and it was the lady that stopped to help my stranded wife and kids.

She welcomed me with open arms into their home and as I humbly thanked her she told me how that it was her good pleasure to help. She told me that she knows that stretch of 315 and how bad that it is in that area. She said that she saw the car pull over and that she wanted to get to them as soon as she could. Again, I thanked her. As I stood there I noticed the big clock and it was now almost 11pm. I hugged my wife and kids and told them that we should say our thanks and goodbyes and be on our way. Our new found Christian friends would not have it. They said that the night is far spent and with the storms outside that they wanted us to stay the night with them.

The woman went on to say that her son and just gotten married and that they had plenty of room. She said with him now gone that it would be nice to have somebody in the house. She poignantly said that she was not doing well being an empty nester. It was late and we were all tired so we decided to take them up on their offer. The boys were ecstatic and were ready to hit the hay. We talked for a bit and then it was off to bed.

I must honestly admit that I did not sleep much through the night. I would pray for a while and then cry. I was in awe as to how that God sent these people to help us. My other reason for my insomnia was that I couldn't help but think about how that I would ever repay these folks for their kindness. I think all told that when I arrived in Columbus that I had maybe 20 dollars to my name. The man paid for the tow and all the other expenses and adamantly refused to let me repay him. All through the night I kept thinking what was it that I could possibly give these people in return for their care.

As soon as I could see daylight coming in around the window blinds I asked God what to do. He knew, and I knew, that just beside my bed was my duffle bag. Inside my duffle bag was my Bible. He laid that scripture on my heart where Jesus talked about people taking in strangers. I got up and began to read and meditate on those verses. It goes like this, "When the Son of man shall come in his glory, and all the holy angels with him, then shall he sit upon the throne of his glory: And before him shall be gathered all nations: and he shall separate them one from another, as a shepherd divideth his sheep from the goats: And he shall set the sheep on his right hand, but the goats on the left. Then shall the King say unto them on his right hand, Come, ye blessed of my Father, inherit the kingdom prepared for you from the foundation of the world: For I was an hungred, and ye gave me meat: I was thirsty, and ye gave me drink: I was a stranger, and ye took me in: Naked, and ye clothed me: I was sick, and ye visited me: I was in prison, and ye came unto me. Then shall the righteous answer him, saying, Lord, when saw we thee an hungred, and fed thee? or thirsty, and gave thee drink? When saw we thee a stranger, and took thee in? or naked, and clothed thee? Or when saw we thee sick, or in prison, and came unto thee? And the King shall answer and say unto them, Verily I say unto you, Inasmuch as ye have done it unto one of the least of these my brethren, ye have done it unto me." (St. Matthew 25:31-40) As I laid there just pondering these scriptures I wondered how that reading this and meditating on it was going to matter to them. Soon I began to hear noises in the downstairs and soon the smell of bacon crowded my nose and I knew that breakfast was on the way.

As we made our way downstairs I could not believe my eyes. This lady had enough food to feed a small Bolivian Army. The menu included fried potatoes, bacon, sausage, eggs, pancakes, waffles (fresh off the waffle iron) fresh fruit, and yes an assortment of dry cereal and oatmeal. Their dining room table was covered. I asked her what she wanted me to do and she asked me to set the table. I started looking for the plates and she pointed to this solid oak cabinet and said, "Dave, in there is our everyday dishes we can use them!" This oak cabinet and their "everyday" dishes were worth more than my car. I just giggled! I couldn't help it.

As we sat down for breakfast the man asked us to bow our heads as he thanked the Lord for us and all that had happened to bring us together. He asked the Lord to bless our food and then we ate and ate! After breakfast I knew that it would be time for us to leave. We all gathered in the family room and they went on and on about how much that they enjoyed us being there. I went up to the room to make sure that we had not left anything and to pray and ask God what to do.

I must admit that I felt horrible because I wondered what I could possibly give them to repay them. As I grabbed my duffle bag to head downstairs I wanted to cry. As I got to the bedroom door God said, "Read it to them!" As I stood there I thought, "Read what to them?" God said read to them about the verses that you read and studied this morning. I thought that there is no way that this is payment enough for what they have done. God said, "Just read it to them."

As I walked downstairs I was shaking all over, inside! I sat down in one of the chairs and I began to tell them about all of the events that led us up to this moment. I told them that I felt greatly humbled because I did not know what I could do to possibly repay them for all that they had done. I then told them that God woke me up this morning with a verse of a scripture and that if it was ok that I would read it for them. They both told me that I could. With tears in my eyes and a quivering voice I read the above verse about others taking people in as strangers. I told them that God was truly the creator of the last 24 hours in our life and they were a Godsend when we needed them most.

After I read the verses to them they both hugged me and said that this scripture reading was more than payment enough. We walked away knowing that the Lord was real and that He cares for those who call Him Lord and Savior.

The B & E

All day long I just kept having a weird feeling come over me as if something was wrong. I was working a 24 hour shift and the feelings just came and went through out the day. As evening settled in the feelings just got worse. I had prayed a little bit about my feelings but never really got an answer. About 11pm I was just overwhelmed by the feeling that something really bad was going to happen and I needed to go home. I called home during the day to see how my wife was and to check on the boys. She never had much to say and so everything didn't seem serious.

I called in a relief person and they arrived at about 12:45am. We chatted for about 5 minutes and I left the station. It only takes me about 5 minutes to get home but on this night that 5 minutes felt like an hour. When I arrived I talked with my wife and asked her if anything seemed out of the ordinary and she told me no. I went upstairs and the boys were fast asleep in their beds. No matter how hard I prayed about this feeling I never really got an answer except for the overwhelming thought that I needed to go home.

It was now about 1:10am and my wife had gone upstairs to go to bed. I turned all the lights off and started upstairs and all of a sudden I heard a light knocking sound on the front door. I stood still to listen for it again and I heard the same knocking. I grabbed my pistol and again stood very still because it was hard to hear this light tapping sound. It sounded like it was the front door so I slowly made my way over to the front door and looked through the little window curtains and there was 4 men standing on my porch.

As they stood on my porch they made no noise. The one had the screen door open and was just barely tapping on the door. There were no vehicles anywhere in sight and as they stood there they were looking through the windows. I was standing just on the other side of the door. I wanted to grab my phone to call 911 but I was afraid to give up my position. As I stood there the knocking stopped and the man that was doing the knocking grabbed the door knob and I could hear that he was trying to turn it.

I knew that if I did not do something that they would just pop the door and come in on me. I reached up and unlocked the door and turned on the porch light and opened the door and confronted them. They all jumped back and the look on their faces was priceless. I did not show my .357 magnum pistol but I hid it behind my back. For a few seconds they did not know what to say. They didn't run or try to get off of my porch.

The one that kept trying the door knob looked at me and asked me if Steve was home. I asked him, "Steve who?" He made up some stupid last name and I told him that Steve did not live here. He said that he was sorry and they filed off my porch very quickly. Within seconds they were gone. I secured the door and left the porch light on. I stayed in the living room for quite some time before I went to bed. Firstly I was keeping watch to see if they would return and secondly I was thanking God for troubling my spirit as He did.

A couple of days later I was talking to a friend of mine who is a local police officer. I told him about the whole event and he started to describe the men for me. I was astonished that he knew their physical description....all 4 of them! I asked him how he knew them and he told me that the police had been receiving calls about 4 men going about the city breaking into homes. He said that the way I described the happenings was exactly how that other citizens explained their experience with them.

I never had another experience with these men and I thank God that He troubled me throughout the day because He knew exactly when they would arrive on my front porch and He got me there just in time to protect my home and family. Well, praise the Lord!

Let it Rain

As I stepped out of the car I looked to the southwest and I knew right then that we had a major storm coming in and that right soon. I hurried into the post office with my package and mailed it from the counter. As I made my way out to the door to exit the building the rain was so hard and forceful I couldn't see out of the glass door. The wind was blowing so hard that I could not budge the door. I realized right then that those of us who "thought" that we were leaving the post office were dreadfully wrong.

As I stood there admiring the fierceness of the storm I noticed that an elderly lady was now joining me. I looked and a young man was now peering out the door wondering when we would be able to leave. Soon a girl about 16 years old was right with our little group of stranded postal customers. Since we could not leave I had a thought come over me. I looked at that teenaged girl and said, "We may have to get in touch with Noah and see if we can get another Ark built." The older lady said that we may have to do just that. The girl had the proverbial deer in the headlights look on her face.

As God began to lead me I asked the girl if she knew about Noah and the Ark. The look on her face was evidence enough that she had no idea what I was talking about. I began to share with her this great story from the book of Genesis in the Bible. I told her that before the great flood that it had never rained from the sky before. She asked me intently, "How can that be possible?" I told her that the Bible says that a mist came up from the Earth and watered the ground. I told her that this was a very key factor in why that when Noah told the people that it was going to rain all they did was mock him. I told her to keep this important Bible fact close at hand.

God said that because man had become so evil and Godless that He would destroy every living thing that lived on the Earth with a great flood. He said that it would rain and that all life would be destroyed. There was at that time a man named Noah who found favor in the sight of God. When it was time to build the Ark, God told Noah that he should build the Ark for the saving of his household. It took Noah 126 years to build it according to Gods specifications.

When the Ark was completed God commanded Noah to put two of each animal on the Ark. So Noah and his wife and 2 sons and their wives prepared the Ark for the trip. As the day came Noah and his family and all of the animals got in the Ark and the Bible says that God shut the door.

As this girl continued to listen as I told her this story our audience had now grown to about 15 people. The rain was coming down so hard that it sounded like a freight train going by outside the post office. It was literally impossible to open the door. I had a captive audience! I told her that now was time for God to fulfill His promise that the water in the form of drops of rain would now start. It wasn't long until the massive Ark would begin to rise off of the ground. I asked her if she could imagine the fear and chaos that must have been going on around that Ark.

I asked her if she knew what color the Ark was. She said it must have been brown because it was made of wood. I told her that she was right with one little exception. I told her that the Ark must have been red too because you know that those people on the outside would have scratched that wood until their fingers bled! She looked down as the thought of that sight settled into her mind. As I continued with the story the others in our group watched on nervously.

I told her that the Ark settled in Mt. Ararat and the waters started to abate. After so many days God sent a raven out of the Ark to see if the waters had dried up. The raven returned. After yet again so many days God sent out a dove. The dove returned later in the evening with an olive branch in her beak. After seven more days he sent out the dove and she never returned. Noah then knew that the waters had abated and that he and his family could now come out of the Ark.

I went on to tell her that Noah and his family and all of the animals came forth out of the Ark with Noah and that he built an altar for the Lord and worshipped God. God then made a covenant with Noah and all mankind that He would never destroy the earth again with a flood. As I continued with telling this girl all of these accounts about this flood and Noah, her eyes were ever on me. Often times she would interject that these things were so hard to believe that they could have happened. I then asked her if she knew why that we see a rainbow in the sky when it rains.

She gave some off set scientific reason for the display. I told her the truth about the rainbow. I told her that God said that He would never destroy the Earth again with a flood and that His promise to us would be in the form of a rainbow in the sky. I told her that this everlasting covenant was between God and man.

Although I knew that this girl comprehended my every word, I also knew that this recounting of this great event was also flooding her mind with unanswered questions. As I looked around at the others I could tell that some were interested and some were really hoping that it would quit raining.

The older lady must have been a Christian because she would add some insight as to what I was trying to tell this girl. She had many questions and I was able to tell her the answers according to the word of God. As we stood there and there seemed to be no break in the storm I told the girl that I wanted to challenge her to do something for the rest of the day. I reiterated the point that God said that He would never destroy the earth again with water. I told her that God promised that the next time that He was going to destroy the Earth with fire that will fall from the sky. And the flood gates opened!

She said, "I don't believe that!" I asked her if she remembered what I said at the beginning of this story about Noah's preaching about water in the form of rain that would fall from the sky. She said, "Yes." I then said that the people in Noah's day did not believe that water would fall from the sky back then and that people of today will not believe that fire is going to fall this time. It doesn't take a mental giant to see that the Earth and the inhabitants therein are growing just as wicked as they were in the days of Noah.

God tells of this date that is fast approaching in the book of II Peter chapter 3 and it goes like this: "This second epistle, beloved, I now write unto you; in both which I stir up your pure minds by way of remembrance: That ye may be mindful of the words which were spoken before by the holy prophets, and of the commandment of us the apostles of the Lord and Saviour: Knowing this first, that there shall come in the last days scoffers, walking after their own lusts, And saying, Where is the promise of his coming? For since the fathers fell asleep, all things continue as they were from the beginning of the creation. For this they willingly are ignorant of, that by the word of God the heavens were of old, and the earth standing out of the water and in the water: Whereby the world that then was, being overflowed with water, perished: But the heavens and the earth, which are now, by the same word are kept in store, reserved unto fire against the day of judgment and perdition of ungodly men." (II Peter 3:1-7)

As I quoted this to her I told her to concentrate on these 8 words. "By the same word are kept in store." God told Noah and the people in his day that due to sin and every form of wickedness that He would destroy the earth with rain and a flood of water. Since the entire world today is full of the same sin and violence God is going to destroy it again; this time it will be by fire! By now the people in that small area by the exit door were no doubt begging for the rain to stop. The girl looked at me and said, "I understand what you're saying but it seems so hard to believe.

I told her that I was not there, but by faith I believe that one event already came to pass and that the other one is getting ready to. It doesn't take an Ivy League graduate to see the horrible shape that the entire world is getting into because of sin and wickedness. As the rain and wind continually pounded the post office I told the girl that I had a challenge for her. I told her to tell the next 15 people that she came in contact with about the story of the Bible scripture in II Peter chapter 3 that gives the details of the event that is soon to come to pass. Tell them that God promised that He would not destroy the Earth with rain again but His choice this time will be fire. Tell them how that sin and iniquity is so great in the world today that God is getting ready to fulfill His word in second Peter chapter 3. Tell them that fire and brimstone will fall like the rain and burn out every living thing.

She stood there with the most profound look on her face. She said, "They will think that I am crazy!" I said, "Well, then you will know how that Noah felt." The people, with the exception of my elderly Bible believer, were pacing the floor and grunting like crazy. Most of them wanted out of that post office but the master of the rain cycle would not let up one bit! I told this girl that she needed to really consider reading the word of God to see what the future holds for mankind. I told her that she should learn about this God and to discover the vastness of His love and plan of salvation. She said, "Ok."

The word "ok" did not make its way one inch around that room and just like it started the rain abruptly stopped! Those 15 or so people almost ran out of that post office. Why? Because the Bible says that most don't believe that the rain fell in Noah's day and they also don't believe that fire will soon fall to this Earth just like God said that it would!

No Blockage Here

Mitchell had been having issues with his gall bladder and test results showed that there was a blockage in the bile ducts. His doctor is from Monroe but his specialist is from Ann Arbor at the U of M. Apparently blockage in the bile ducts can be serious so an appointment was made for surgery. As we prepared to leave Monroe that morning my mom was sitting in her chair and we were discussing the surgery. As I turned to walk away to leave for the hospital she said to me, "There will be no surgery this morning!"

My mom is our spiritual leader in our family. She got saved by the Lord at the age of 12 at the foot of her mailbox on an old country road in a place called New Tazewell, Tennessee. She has lived for God all of these years and has truly walked her salvation not just talked it. When she said that there would be no surgery I knew that she had spent time with the Lord in prayer. My mom seldom made any statement like that unless she was sure that God was in the works.

When we got to Ann Arbor we had a good size group of us with Mitchell. When they took him back to prep him for surgery they assured us that we could see him before he went under. We waited for about a half an hour and they brought him out in the bed. The nurse said we were delayed because they actually had to fly a doctor in from Chicago that morning to do the surgery. As we sat there talking to Mitchell several student doctors and several residents joined in with us. Just then another nurse came out and said that the doctor from Chicago had arrived and that she was preparing for surgery. She said that we could spend just another minute or two with Mitchell and then she was taking him back.

As we always try to do....we had prayer. As we all circled his bed we joined hands. Several of the doctors and students joined hands with us for the prayer. I must say that that truly blessed my soul to see those doctors and students join hands with us. As we bowed our heads we invited the Lord to come into our midst and to be with Mitchell during the surgery. We asked God to be with the doctors and to guide their hands and to bless them in their work for humanity. As every head was bowed we could feel the Holy Spirit of God moving about the room. It was a powerful prayer time! As we finished the prayer we asked for this petition to be granted in the name of Jesus. The nurse came and got him and took him back.

We were not exactly certain how long that this would take all I know was that God answered somebody's prayer! Mitchell was only back there about 15 minutes and the nurse came back out and said, "There's no blockage!" She said, "We took him to recovery and when he wakes up you can take him home!" Well, praise the Lord! In about a half an hour Mitchell was awake and we took him home after a bit of time.

The nurse did say that the doctor from Chicago was a little perturbed but she was certain that she would get over it. When we got home we walked in and my mom asked,

"Well, how'd it go?" I smiled and said, "You know how it went." She told me then that God showed her before we even left Monroe that there was no blockage. I thank God for His mercy!

Bishop Milton Jackson

Brother Milton Jackson was a Bishop of a local Pentecostal Church here in Monroe. He was a well respected man of God who truly loved the Lord. Brother Milton would always ask me if I was staying faithful to the Lord. He had a genuine concern for people, wanted people to know that the Lord loved them, and that they need to be saved. He and his wife Ann worked very hard in our community proclaiming the good news of Jesus Christ.

Word came that Brother Milton received that call from the portals of glory and that it was his time to go to his home in heaven. The news struck me hard because I really loved him and I knew first hand all of the hard work that he was dedicated to. Brother Milton was also a dedicated husband and family man so I knew also that he would be missed by them too. I made some calls and found out about his "Going Home Celebration" and made preparations to go.

Stewart Road Church of God is a very large church and has ample parking for a celebration like Brother Milton's. As my wife and I arrived we saw a literal sea of cars and people filing into the church. It was very moving. Since my wife and I were on our way out of town for another family engagement we had purposed ourselves to just visit with his wife, Sister Ann Jackson, and then be on our way. As we entered the church we began to inquire the whereabouts of Sister Jackson.

Her son told us that she had not yet arrived and that we should stand right by the rear main entrance doors to the church so that we would not miss her. So, that is what we did. As we stood there we watched as the masses of people came into the church but we didn't see his wife. After almost an hour went by I told my wife that we might have to leave and then just see her later. I really didn't want to leave but we had to. My wife asked me if we could stay just a little longer. I told her that we could and she stayed by the doors but I went over by the drinking fountain about 20 feet away.

Although I was physically there at the church my mind and heart were troubled about something else going on in my life. I had a great need that nobody else but God and I knew about and it was troubling me. As I stood there by that water fountain I just kept asking God to help me with this problem. As I stood there I also tried to keep a visual on the door to see if Sister Ann would come in. I was trying to juggle my feelings in my mind about my friend who went home to be with the Lord and I was also dealing with something that I knew that I just couldn't fix.

As I pondered my feelings I recalled that so many times how that Brother Milton told me that God cares. Just as I entertained those precious words of Godly wisdom those rear double doors opened up and 5 men in the exact same black suits came walking in single file. They walked very slow and solemn as they made their way across the floor. As they walked in I fixed my eyes on the third man in the line. He was tall and bald and looked like he was on business for the King. God told me to go and join myself to that man and to ask him to pray for me and the problem that was bothering me. I stood there frozen and didn't move!

As they made their way towards that main entrance door to the sanctuary God again impressed me to go and have that man pray for me. I totally quenched the spirit and did not go. Again God told me to go and I just stood there and did not move. As I watched all five of them made their way into the main part of the sanctuary and I knew right then and there that I had disobeyed God by not joining myself with that man.

With the hurt of Brother Milton dying, the problem that I was facing, and now I totally had disobeyed God I wanted to scream. I then determined myself that I would go and look for that man. He couldn't be found! I looked and looked as if he was a missing child of mine and he was not to be found. My heart was broken and racing at the same time. How could I have done this since the power of God was so great leading me to talk to this man? I was in total despair.

I believe that God will put angels in our path and if we disobey His leading spirit then it is us that will inevitably lose the blessing. This is what that I was sure that I had done. As I made my way back towards where my wife was at the entrance doors I was greatly saddened. I could have busted into tears but I didn't want to. My sadness was more about the fact that I had disobeyed God and not my problem. I walked back down the hallway that leads out of the church and as I passed by the main entrance to the sanctuary I looked down the main aisle and there he was.

Just about half way down to where the altar was I saw that man standing in the aisle talking to a family member. I made up my mind that I would not quench the spirit of God again. God in all of His mercy and compassion gave me another chance to go and see that man. As I slowly made my way down the isle I was trembling and tears were streaming down my face. As I got to him he turned and fixed his eyes on me. I thought that I would just melt right there in front of him. He turned to face me and I extended my hand to shake his. When he took my hand the power of God shot right through me. I knew right then that God wanted me to talk to him.

As he continued to hold onto my hand I told him how that I watched as he entered the Church. I told him how that the Lord had told me to go and ask him to pray for me. I went on to say that I greatly quenched the Spirit of God and with tears in my eyes I asked him to forgive me. I told him that I was facing something and that I really needed help from the Lord. I told him that I believed that I ruined my chances of getting Godly intervention since I disobeyed God's leadership. Throughout these few seconds he never took his eyes off of me.

I never told him what my situation was. I stood there, asked him to remember me in prayer, and thanked him. As I turned to walk away he still had a hold of my hand. He never let go; moreover, he pulled me back around and brought me right up to him and he started to pray right there in that aisle. He began to ask God to remember me and to bless me and then he told God "exactly" what I had need of. He was trembling and it felt like that I had hold of a live electric wire. The power of God was flowing through him and running through me too.

After a few minutes of prayer he finished by thanking the Lord for His goodness and mercy. He hugged me and all fear and anxiety with regard to my situation left me. I left there knowing that God is a God of love and mercy and even when I fail Him sorely He still cares and still loves me!

Raymond Bragg

Raymond and Janet Bragg lived on South Raisinville Road in Monroe. I am not sure how that they and my mom and dad became friends but it was a very long time ago. They were as close to being an Aunt and Uncle to me as any of my real ones. Janet was a Bus Driver and Raymond worked in a metal pickling company. Due to the lead content in the metals that Raymond worked with he contracted serious lead poisoning and took a medical retirement at an early age. Janet continued driving the bus and he became a handyman doing little fix up jobs for people. They have a son, Raymond and a daughter Melissa.

Over the years Raymond would get sick from his work illness and he would get hospitalized. At times he would be in critical condition. He would seemingly bounce back and be good as gold. He would joke around that God was not ready for him yet and that the devil was afraid that he would take over. He always had a light hearted outlook on eternity. This time, as it relates to this story, Raymond would not be coming home.

"Uncle" Raymond was really sick this time. He was in the ICU and he was not bouncing back like he normally did. As his condition grew worse he got to the point where he was no longer responding at all to treatment. We were all worried that without a miracle that he might not make it. He could no longer communicate with the medical staff and family. It was really sad to see him struggling for his life.

That Sunday morning my dad left the house and went to see him in the ICU. He and Raymond were closer than many blood brothers. My mom and I left the house and went to Sunday school. After we got to the church my mom told me that they were going to have special prayer with me and that they wanted me to go and see Uncle Raymond and have prayer with him. The Pastor, Brother Delmar Moore, called the entire congregation up to the altar for special prayer and the entire church made their way up. Church service had not even started yet. As I knelt down in the center of the altar everyone just gathered around me and anointed me with oil and laid their hands on me. And the church prayed!

After the prayer was over my mom told me to go and to do whatever that God laid on my heart to do. So I got in my car and headed for the hospital. When I got there I went to the ICU and when the big doors opened I saw my dad standing near the nurse's station. I walked over to him and as I looked to my right I could see the room where Uncle Raymond was lying in bed.

What happened next I can hardly believe except that it was God moving on his behalf! From where I was standing it was about 20 feet to his room door and it was open. I could see him through the large glass wall and he was lying in the bed and he was facing away from me as if he was looking out the window. As I started talking to my dad Uncle Raymond heard my voice and turned his head and opened his eyes and looked through the glass wall at me! Needless to say this was the only sign of life that he had shown in three days. I knew right then that God was in the works.

After talking to my dad for just a minute I went into his room. He had turned his head back towards the window as if to be looking outside his room and was not awake or responding. I said hello to everybody as they commented about him looking for me when he heard my voice out in the hallway. I stood there at his bedside not really knowing what to say or do. I began to silently ask the Lord what He wanted me to do. Nothing came to me. As I prayed all I could do was ask God to give me the very thing to say that would help. As I held his hand I patiently waited on God.

As the room remained silent I kept asking the Lord what to do. I try to wait on the Lord because under His leadership I know that the right thing will be done according to His will. All of a sudden God began to lead me to the Bible accounting of Samson in the book of Judges.

Samson's mother was barren and unable to have children. She wanted a child so an angel of the Lord appeared unto her and told her that she would have a son. The biblical accounting goes like this, "And the angel of the Lord appeared unto the woman, and said unto her, Behold now, thou art barren, and barest not: but thou shalt conceive, and bear a son. Now therefore beware, I pray thee, and drink not wine nor strong drink, and eat not any unclean thing: For, lo, thou shalt conceive, and bear a son; and no razor shall come upon his head: for the child shall be a Nazarite unto God from the womb: and he shall begin to deliver Israel out of the hand of the Philistines." (Judges 13:3-5) This proclamation was made and the angel said that Samson would be a Nazarite up to the day of his death.

The covenant that God made with Samson's mother was that no razor would come upon his head and thus his strength would be gone. Not because his hair was cut but that this was a covenant with God about this son and that it should not be broken. As the story goes on Samson meets a harlot named Delilah and she tricks Samson into telling her where his strength came from. Samson finally told her that if his hair was cut then he would be as normal men. She had it cut while he slept and he lost his strength and the Philistines plucked out his eyes and put him in prison.

While Samson was in prison his hair began to grow again. Soon it would be time that they would bring Samson out into the large arena to make sport with him. As Samson was led to the arena by a young boy he asked for the lad to let him stand between the pillars that held up the entire arena. "And Samson said unto the lad that held him by the hand, Suffer me that I may feel the pillars whereupon the house standeth, that I may lean upon them." (Judges 16:26) Even though Samson was blind he knew that the arena would be full because they hated him.

As Samson stood there with a hand on each of the two pillars he knew that he could not do this on his own so he called out to the one that he knew could help him. "And Samson called unto the Lord, and said, O Lord God, remember me, I pray thee, and strengthen me, I pray thee, only this once, O God, that I may be at once avenged of the Philistines for my two eyes." (Judges 16:28) Samson knew that he was going to die but he remembered who he could call on in his time of need. As I knelt there holding Uncle Raymond's hand I was telling him that he needed to call on the same God.

As I knelt there I told Raymond again that he needed to call on the Lord for strength and mercy. I then started to pray. I was really asking God to give him the opportunity to call on him just this once. I asked the Lord to speak to his heart so that Raymond could be sure that he was saved and ready to meet the Lord in a free pardon of sin. As I prayed I could really feel the power of God in the ICU room. As I finished the prayer I asked the Lord again to do this for Raymond for His glory and His honor. I then said, "Lord we ask these things in the name of Jesus!" As soon as I said "Jesus" the heart monitor went flat line. Uncle Raymond stepped from the walks of this life into eternity.

There was a peace that came over me and everyone in that room. Raymond did not want to be on life support. I believe that everything that happened that morning was ordained by God. As the family made funeral arrangements they asked me if I would sing for him during the service. I was greatly humbled. Again, I sought God as to the song that He would have me sing. God so appropriately laid on my heart the song, "Wonderful Peace."

The song is on page 290 in the Red Church Hymnal. It has five verses but verse 2 reminded me of Raymond. "What a treasure I have in this wonderful peace, Buried deep in the heart of my soul. So secure that no power can mine it away, While the years of eternity roll." This is the chorus, "Peace! Peace! wonderful peace, Coming down from the father above; Sweep over my spirit forever I pray, In fathomless billows of love."

The Black Dog

My oldest son Mitchell and his friend Eric McLaughlin have been best friends since kindergarten. They went through school together, been in each others weddings, and traveled together. They both work in law enforcement. One hobby that they share is riding motorcycles. This miracle of God is about a ride that they took one afternoon.

They turned off of North Telegraph Road onto Eric's road and as they sped up on their motorcycles a very large black dog came bolting out of the ditch right into their path. As they both nearly laid their bikes on the pavement; they were very fortunate to have missed running into this large dog. They drove the short distance down to Eric's house and sat there on their bikes trying to calm down. They both took off their helmets and sat quietly in the driveway.

After a few seconds they both decided that they would travel back down to the area where they encountered that dog so that they could shoot it. They both carry guns so in their moment of anxiety over the near miss they thought going back down to the scene would be the next best step to take. Neither I'm sure would ever bring harm to any dog but in the heat of the moment it seemed like the thing to do. So, they donned their helmets and headed down to where the dog came up out of that ditch.

As soon as they neared the place of the incident they did not see any dog. What they did see was an older man on the ground near his mailbox unresponsive. They both ditched their bikes and helmets and went to the aid of the downed citizen. A quick patient survey showed that the man was in full cardiac arrest. Without hesitation Eric started mouth-to-mouth and Mitchell began doing chest compressions. With CPR in progress the Fire and EMS crews were summoned. After they arrived they took over patient care. The man had a pulse and was attempting to breathe on his on his own.

After the man was loaded into the ambulance they quickly rushed him to our local hospital. As Mitchell and Eric stood there they began to question the bystanders and neighbors about a big black dog. The witnesses that lived near the scene told them that they did not know of anyone who had such an animal. As law enforcement officers both Mitchell and Eric have been trained in the technique of searching for clues and evidence at a scene. They looked over the area where the dog came out of the ditch and there were no dog tracks and/or any other signs of a dog being there. Nobody was able to give them any information with regard to ownership of the dog.

After several days we found out that the patient went home with no complications from the full cardiac arrest. After interviewing the patient he said that he did not know of any large black dogs in that area. If that dog that Mitchell and Eric saw would not have scared them in the way that he did they may not have had occasion to go back down to find a man in need of life saving help!

The Chicken Broth

My dad had been sick for some time and he was in the VA Hospital in Ann Arbor. For many reason we had not talked in about seven years. My Aunt called to tell us that he was not doing well and that we should come and see him. I decided to travel to Ann Arbor to see him even though I was not sure if he would want to see me. Often times when the spirit is willing the flesh is weak. My first thought was that I would try to go and see him and if I was thrown out I could rest in the assurance that I tried. I was on my way!

I got to see him but the visit was not really pretty. Words were exchanged and I felt extremely uncomfortable about the visit. I knew that I had not done anything to merit my treatment but I was trying to be the better person. As I left the hospital I knew that he really didn't care much about my visit. Some times God will allow us to enter into the lion's den for a visit to give Him the opportunity to show who is really in charge. I can say that this was truly one of those times.

My dad had cancer and was really bad. After a few days my Aunt called again to tell us that he was worse and that he had not eaten in a few days. That news cut me to the very marrow of my bones. If there is one thing that I can't stand is hearing that somebody is hungry. It was about 11 pm when she called me that night. I was just getting ready to go to bed but I didn't know how much sleep that I would get.

Jesus tells us in St. Matthew chapter 5 and verse 43, "Ye have heard that it hath been said, Thou shalt love thy neighbor, and hate thine enemy. But I say unto you, Love your enemies, bless them that curse you, do good to them that hate you, and pray for them which despitefully use you, and persecute you; That ye may be the children of your Father which is in heaven: for he maketh his sun to rise on the evil and on the good, and sendeth rain on the just and on the unjust." (St. Matthew 5:43-45) Even though in my flesh I did not want to pray for my dad I knew that this is what God wanted me to do.

From 11 pm that night until I saw the sun coming through the windows the next morning I prayed. I knew that after a few days of no food that my dad would be hungry. I knew my dad well enough to know that when it was time to eat that he was usually more than ready. My dad was not really the "snacking" kind of eater. He was a three meal a day meat and potatoes kind of guy. He usually made no bones about it when it was time to grub!

As I prayed I began to run it through my mind what he could possibly eat. As I prayed I began to think about how that the hospitals are notorious for serving chicken noodle soup. I began to really ask God to consider how hungry that he must be and that even a little to eat would be better than nothing. I remember vividly that I asked the Lord to help him just enough that he would be able to have some chicken broth. I told the Lord that even if it didn't have any chunks of meat in it at least let him have some broth. I prayed that some warm chicken broth with just a little salt would help him. As I begged God for this favor my tears fell like rain.

As I prayed through the night I remember telling God that many people are praying for or seeking fortunes. I told God that many are seeking fame. Many are looking for the answers to life's many problems. With my whole heart though, I prayed for an enemy to get the blessing of 4 ounces of soup broth. When it started getting daylight I looked at the clock and it was about 6 am. I laid there until just after 7am and my phone rang. I answered it and it was my Aunt with an update from the VA.

My Aunt told me that the nurses didn't know what happened through the night. They said that my dad was awake and in his right mind. They told her that he slept all night and had no problems on the midnight shift. She said that even though he had not eaten in more than 2 days he had eaten this morning. I asked my Aunt if she knew what he had for breakfast. I quietly whispered that my heart's desire was that God would help him enough that he would be able to eat just 4 ounces of chicken broth. My Aunt said that he had surprised them all.

She went on to tell me that he had 2 eggs, bacon, toast, jelly, and was on his second cup of coffee. I could have jumped out of my skin. Through the night I prayed for so little and God came on the scene in such a profound way. My dad never talked to me again and it wasn't long until he died. I am glad that God knows my heart and even though he considered me a great enemy, the God of Abraham, Isaac, and Jacob gave me leave to pray for him. What a joy it is when God comes on the scene.

Ricky

The Portsmouth Hospital was about a half an hour away from Vanceburg, Kentucky, and I wanted to be careful not to let time slip away from me with regard to visiting hours. My wife's Aunt Janet was in the hospital and I wanted to go and visit with her for a bit. I got dressed and headed to the hospital. When I got there she was awake and they were just bringing supper. We chatted and enjoyed a good visit. She told me that she was getting discharged the next day and that she was feeling much better.

I had taken my Bible up to her room but I didn't really feel as though the Lord had laid any scriptures on my heart. Janet's husband, Bill was the Pastor of two churches. They both had professed Christ as their personal Savior and I felt my spirit bearing witness with theirs that they were children of God. It was such a great joy to be around them. As I got ready to leave the Lord impressed on me to read the eighth chapter of the book of Isaiah. It's about God's exhortation to look to Him and live for Him and not idols.

After I finished reading this we had prayer. I told Aunt Janet that I was not praying for her salvation because she had already made preparations to meet the Lord. I did tell her though that I was praying that God would touch her and to be with her. Just then a thought came over me that

I wanted to quickly share with her. I said, "You know I don't have to worry about you because you are already saved but I believe that there is someone out there that does need to hear the good news about the Lord!" She said, "I do too." I gave her a hug and was on my way.

After going through town I made my way to the new bridge that I could cross on my way back to Vanceburg. As I got out of town the big bridge came into view. Just then it started to rain and as I looked towards the turn off for the bridge I saw a man standing there hitch hiking. I kinda giggled and thought to myself, "Lord, is that him?" No sooner than I thought that, God said, "Pick him up." As I got to where he was standing it started to rain a little harder. My heart was pounding because this was the very person that Aunt Janet and I were talking about that needed to hear about the Lord.

I pulled off the road and he opened my door and asked me, "Are you the preacher?" I told him no! I was not in a suit. I had no name tags on that said clergy or chaplain. I was driving and old grey van that had no indication on it that I was there on business for the Lord. He was getting wet as the rain steadily fell on him and he said, "Sir, I am wet and I don't want to get your van wet!" I told him not to worry about my old van and he got in.

He went on to tell me that his name was Ricky and that he was from Firebrick, Kentucky. Firebrick is just one of the countless little towns in the hills of Kentucky along the Ohio River. He said that he had been in Portsmouth and without a ride home that he would just try to walk or hitch hike. He said that he wasn't really worried that much about the walk until it started to rain. Well, for now we were riding in style and we were heading to Firebrick.

As we rode I began to tell him about visiting my Aunt Janet at the hospital. I told him how that I had read from my Bible for her and how that we had prayed. I told him that I knew from her witness that she was a Christian and on her way home to glory. I told Ricky how that we had also prayed that somewhere out on the road on my way back to Vanceburg that there would be somebody who needed to hear the good news of Jesus Christ. With everything in me I knew that God had put him there for that reason. With his heart breaking and his eyes pooled up with tears I knew that he really needed God in his life.

As we drove I told Ricky of many of the good things that God had done for me and how that he too could accept the Lord and His mercy. As we neared the turnoff to Firebrick, Ricky told me that I could just drop him off and he would walk the rest of the way. I told him that if he didn't mind that there was no reason to walk and that I would give him a ride all the way home. With teary eyes he agreed to the ride.

As we finally pulled in front of his home he thanked me. I told him that it was I that was thankful that God allowed our paths to cross. I told him that the Lord loved him and that I did too. I told him to seek God for His love and salvation before it was too late. As he moved to get out of the van he reached over and shook my hand. I sat there as he walked up to the house and then went inside. It wasn't long before I made it back to Vanceburg. I was absolutely reeling over the fact that as I went on business for the King in order to maybe say or do something to help a family member I met a lost man who needed the Lord.

The Christmas Tree

We lived on a small dead end street called Woodville Avenue. My dad, mom, and four kids lived in a small 3 bedroom house. Christmas has always been my favorite holiday due in part to how my mom always took nothing seemingly and turned it into a grand celebration. This year, back in the late 60's would prove to be no different. My mom has been busy since about May getting ready for that special morning. We were typical kids just counting days and wearing out the Christmas catalogs.

As the time would grow near to Christmas morning we started seeing all of the Christmas trees for sale at the little roadside lots. What was out of the norm was that my dad was not stopping to get a tree. Back then the only two stores that we had for shopping were K-Mart and Bargain City. Each time that we would all head to one of the stores we would pass by the place next to K-Mart where we always got our tree. This failure to stop and get one was really causing a stir with me.

With Christmas only a couple of weeks away I was panicked. When I asked my mom about us not having a tree yet she simply made up some long version story that still left me wondering. It wouldn't be until many years later that I would find out the real reason why. With only about a week and a half from Christmas morning left, my mom and dad told us that after supper that we were going to go to Bargain City to do some shopping. I was really tickled because I thought that we were now finally going to get our tree.

It had been snowing and the wind was blowing and it was really cold that night. Driving conditions were bad and as we drove to Bargain City there were few cars out on the road. We already had about eight to ten inches of snow on the ground and the scenes were very picturesque. Every turn and every glimpse that the eye could behold was like an artist rendition of Christmas past. We scurried into Bargain City and shopped for about an hour. When we came out of the store our old Chevy Carry-All was completely covered with snow.

It's important to note that when we came to Bargain City we did not drive by the place where we always got our Christmas trees. My dad drove a different route. When we started home I wondered if this night would be our night to get the tree. As we traveled south on North Monroe Street we met up with only one or two cars. Due to the storm not many people had ventured out. There seemed to be a very eerie feeling in the air that night!

As we drove south towards K-Mart and headed toward the Christmas tree lot just south of K-Mart I noticed that there was a strange mist in the air. Since the roads were bad my dad didn't drive very fast. As we neared the intersection of North Monroe Street and Stewart Roads I noticed that there were no other cars on the road. There were only a few scant tracks from other cars but for the most part the new snow lay untouched. As we sat at the traffic light I couldn't help but see how that the Christmas tree lot was lit up by the strings of lights. As the light changed my dad continued south on North Monroe Street and we were only about two blocks away from the tree lot. As we neared the lot my heart raced.

North Monroe Street makes a curve to the right just after K-Mart so it is impossible to see towards downtown Monroe until you actually go past the K-Mart entrance and past the Christmas tree lot. As my dad drove we were right at the entrance to the Christmas tree lot but he did not slow down and made no indication that he was going to stop. As I stared at the trees my heart sank as he drove right on by. As we passed the entrance I wanted to cry. I did make one little observation as we drove by. My mom was looking towards the Christmas tree lot very intently. I could see it in her face that she really wanted to stop. And my dad drove right on by.

As we drove I noticed that there were no other cars on the road. As I said earlier, it was really a weird feeling because it seemed as if we were the only one out that night. As we rounded the curve I could see into the downtown area of the City of Monroe. The fog and mist was everywhere and the street lights only enhanced their appearance. As I looked ahead about fifty yards I noticed that a large garbage can was right in the road right in the lane that we were in. It was covered with snow and there were no car tracks or any other disturbances around it. As my dad slowed down I noticed a big smile on my moms face.

As we got closer the headlights began to break through the steady falling snow enough for me to see that it was not a garbage can......it was a Christmas tree! As my dad came to a stop right in front of the tree I could have screamed. He said, "Well look Santy Claus dropped off a tree for us." My mom had another answer for this great gift. My dad got out of the car and began to look it over. It was not damaged and appeared to have been there for some time. Since there were no car tracks around and no footprints around it he figured that it must have fallen off of somebody's car. It was completely covered with snow but it was a gem in my eyes. My dad just sat there looking at it and started to shake all of the snow from it. He wanted to sit there for a minute to see if anybody would come to claim it.

As we sat there right in the middle of the road we noticed that no cars were even on the road at all. The whole scene was very tranquil and heaven sent. After a bit my dad just loaded it into the car and we took it home. It was one of the greatest Christmas trees that I ever had in my life.

After more than thirty years later my mom and I were reminiscing about Christmas time and some of the more memorable ones. While talking I brought up how that I remembered this story of the tree in the road. She said that she too remembered this story very vividly. She told me that when we made that trip by the tree lot that night that she knew in her heart that if God did not make a way somehow for us to get a tree that night that we probably would not get one.

With tears in both of our eyes she told me how that as we were right in front of that lot that night there was no way for us to have a tree that year. She said as she looked one more time at those trees sitting there she asked the Lord to make a way for us to have a tree. I remember that look from that night. As we drove past the tree lot and my mom turned her eyes away from it is when we rounded that corner and saw the miracle of that simple prayer that night for a Christmas tree.

She told me that my dad had been out of work for some time and that we were broke. She had been shopping for us since about May so she had that covered. It may seem odd that a tree was without our financial reach but God made a way. According to Wilbur and Peg Matthes from the Matthes Christmas tree farm in Ida, Michigan, a tree only cost about $3.00 dollars back then. Christmas would have came and went that year in the absence of a tree but God knew how important that it was to me and He brought another Christmas miracle to pass!

The Jumper Cables

Over the years I have had a several cars that for whatever reason needed to be jump started. Additionally, I have always had jumper cables that were either broke or not very reliable. The one person that would give me a jump was my dad. He would grumble somewhat and then he would come to wherever I was broke down and do his magic. A few times he came to my aid and when he saw my jumper cables he would give me a hard time. Finally he told me it was time to get some real jumper cables.

I was working at a steel mill and this set the stage for my dad and his quest for me to be successful in my endeavor to get new cables. It was not that I was making sufficient money to buy a fancy pair. In his mind that would be too easy. He said that I could "make" a pair that would exceed any that I could buy. And my journey begins.

My dad told me to check to see if the company had a policy that allowed their employees an opportunity to "have" certain things from the company on a "property pass." I checked it out and they did allow certain things to be taken. My dad was overjoyed! He told me that in a steel mill that they use welding machines and they use welding cables like a hamburger joint uses buns. He then said that due to the nature of working around hot metal and sharp objects that the welding cables get damaged. He said this is where we hit pay dirt. Of course I am looking around like the deer in the headlights!

He told me to put the word out that I needed two pieces of welding cable at least ten feet long. He said that when part of the cable gets damaged that they have to throw away the whole thing. He said most of the time there is at least ten feet that is not damaged. He told me that welding cable makes the best battery cables. It wasn't long until I had two pieces of welding cable sitting in a box in my office with my name on it. I was still curious how this was going to work. You would have thought my dad won the lottery!

I called him to tell him that I had my wires. He then told me to go to the hardware store and buy two red heavy duty clamps and two black heavy duty ones. He told me what kind of nuts and bolts that I would need to finish putting them together. So off to the hardware store I went. I bought all of the stuff he said that I needed and I made arrangements to go to his house and complete the mission. I got to his house and he was waiting for me as if I had just returned from a worldwide safari and he hadn't seen me in years.

Down we went to the far garage with our wares and he told me that if I had everything that we would be done in a few short minutes. He was right! After less than a half an hour I was the proud new father of the best looking jumper cables born on that day in Monroe County. My dad was so proud I thought he was going to pass out cigars to all of the neighbors. As I wiped them off and started to put them in my trunk my dad said, "Now! You have a pair of jumper cables that will never wear out and you can keep those forever!" Famous last words I'll say!

For about a week or so I just kept wondering when my car was going to die so I could use my new cables. I was so proud of them you would have thought that I would have hung them from my rear view mirror! And then it happened.....kinda! I went to the Kroger store on North Monroe Street to do some shopping and when I came out of the store there was a car near me and the young girl had the hood up on her car. I walked over to see if I could help and she said that her car was always giving her trouble and that it wouldn't start. I went to my trunk and whipped out me new cables as if they were made by Rolex!

I hooked up her car and she got inside and it fired right up. She got out and thanked me and told me that it was so embarrassing how that her car was always needing a jump start. I told her to just let it charge up for a minute. I said that of course so that I could take a minute or two to tell her about my new born jumper cables. I told her that I too had many problems with my car not wanting to start and that is why that I made myself the new cables that she just used. I told her that I would never need another pair now that I had this new pair. She again thanked me and I walked away carrying my cables to my car.

As I got to my car I looked back over to her car and she was just getting ready to close her hood. As I opened my trunk to put my cables in God said, "Go give them to her!" My first reaction was, "What?" The Lord again said, "Go and give them to her." I literally stood there not able to move and was not able to even drop those jumper cables into my trunk. I looked over at that girl again and for the third time God told me to go and give them to her. I thought about all of the times that I will need them and all the time and effort that I had spent getting these together and now the Lord wants me to just give them to this young girl!

As she looked at me she smiled and opened her door to get in. I yelled over and told her to wait a minute. She stood there as I shut my trunk and with my cables in my hands made my way over to her car. I told her that I wanted her to have the cables in case she needed a jump again.

As she stood there her eyes pooled up with tears. She said, "But these are your new ones and you may need them." I told her that God had laid it on my heart to give them to her and that I wanted her to have them. She said she had no money to pay me and I told her that she didn't owe me a thing. She shut her car off and opened her trunk and I put them in for her. She got in and her car started up and she drove away. From that day until the writing of this book I have not had one occasion where I needed to have my car jump started using a pair of jumper cables. God is surely good!

Tennessee and Back on Eighty Bucks

I was really in a low spot, in the eyes of the rest of the world, but that did not sway me much. It was summer time and many of my family had planned to go to Tennessee for about a week. I really wanted to go but did not know if I could afford it. My car had four bald tires so bad that the steel belts were sticking out and would flap as I drove down the road. I have three sons and of course they were chomping at the bit to go. I seldom ever talked money to them and I tried to make it look like we were rich. So, with my three sons, eighty dollars in my pocket, and a quarter of a tank of gas we joined the caravan heading south.

We stopped in Ohio for a bathroom and fuel up break and my sister watched as I put five dollars in my tank. She asked me why that I did not fill up and I told her that five was all that I needed. She rolled her eyes, and her bank roll, and got in her car. So we were on the road again. We got gas and our usual snacks and headed for Tennessee.

When we got to New Tazewell, Tennessee, I had less than a quarter of a tank of gas in my car. As we pulled into town the boys and I were hungry so we ate a burger and then it was off to my grandparent's house. While there we did our usual things like hunting and riding around the country side. One morning when I got up I started my car to go into town and I noticed smoke pouring out from under the hood. I had an engine fire! I jumped out and opened the hood and all of the wiring around the battery and starter was burning. Fortunately I was able to put them out.

I told the boys that we were probably stranded now without a mode of transportation. After about an hour I decided to go back out and look the car over. It looked ok with the exception of all the burnt wires. I decided to try and start my car and it fired right up. The boys and I loaded up and we went to town. While in town we ate and went to the store and cruised around as if we were in a new car. We gave little thought to what had happened. We picked up some pop and usual goodies and went back to my grandparents.

The next morning we went to the Flea Market on the other side of town. I wondered if the car would even start and if it did could we go that far. It did and we went to the Flea Market and ate and had a ball. All this time my family was wondering how in the world all of this was taking place. Each time anybody brought up the subject about the condition of my tires, the car fire, and my money situation; I just told them that this was one of my many "faith" trips that I was on.

From the time that we even started talking about going down south the boys mentioned getting fireworks. I didn't lose sleep over it but I wondered how in the world I was going to be able to afford fireworks. They are so expensive and the markup on them is maniacal. Well, as my fears would have it, they wanted to know when we were going to Maynardville. The drive time to get to the fireworks store in Maynardville, Tennessee, from New Tazewell,

Tennessee, is about thirty-five minutes. Without a word about money we planned to go the next day.

We headed to Maynardville and when we got there I thought that the place was closed. The boys freaked out. I told them that we would check to see if anybody was in the store. All three of the boys were excited to get inside but Matthew the middle son was bound and determined to be in the store first. As we filed in there were no other customers in the store. A middle-aged woman was sitting at the counter and when Matthew walked in he said to her, "We are here to get some fire crackers!" She looked up and over the counter at him and said, "With your accent you don't sound like you are from around here." Matthew said, "No, we are from Michigan. She asked, "Is that so?" Matthew said, "Yep." She then told him, "Well, I just want you to know that today is your lucky day. Anybody from Michigan in the store today can buy one and get three free!" I could have cried.

We spent eighteen dollars and walked out with three full grocery bags of fireworks. When we got back to New Tazewell the boys ran and told everybody what the lady said. They all knew that there was no way that I had the money to buy that many fireworks considering the amount of money that I had brought and the amount that I had already spent. We set off fireworks for three days and still brought some home with us.

The day before we left we were going back into town to hang out and to get something to eat. After we got to the shopping plaza I again noticed smoke pouring out from under my hood. I opened the hood and again my electrical wiring was burning. I was able to put it out before it spread too badly. As we sat there I thought of who would be able to come from my grandparent's house to get us. While we shopped, the car cooled down. I thought that I would just try to start it to see if she would crank over. The car fired up and we drove back to my grandparents.

When we pulled up the boys told everybody again how that the car caught on fire and how that they were afraid that it would blow up. The wiring was burnt just a bit worse from the first fire but it was running ok. Most of my family asked me how I was going to get home. I told them that so far my trip was based on faith and that the Lord would see me home.

The week had flown by and we had more fun than if we would have been on a fancy cruise ship. We loaded up the car and said our goodbyes and we were Michigan bound. Many in our company and many at my grandparents either made fun of me or told me not to try going home in my car. I told them that we would be just fine. We traveled home in style and made it without a glitch. With four bald tires, two engine fires, eighty bucks in my pocket, and a fireworks miracle we had one of the best trips to Tennessee that I have ever ventured on. The boys never knew how much or little money that we had. They enjoyed themselves and lived like kings for a week in Tennessee.

$8.37

My wife and my three sons and I lived in the City of Monroe on South Roessler Street. We lived on the corner of Front Street and South Roessler. The boys attended Riverside Elementary school that was located just two blocks north of our home. They had to cross the bridge over the River Raisin to get to the school. It was a busy intersection where we lived with all of the usual hustle and bustle noises associated with living near a busy intersection.

On this particular day neither my wife nor I had to work. We just sat around relaxing waiting for the boys to get home from school. As my wife sat on the couch she had a perplexing grimace on her face. I asked her what was wrong and she told me that we did not have anything for supper, that the boys would be home soon, and when they get home they are usually ready to eat. I asked her if we had anything at all for supper. She said we have a loaf of bread!

As we sat there I checked the time and it was about 2:45pm and I knew that they would be home at about 3:15. As the time grew closer the boys' mother got more and more anxious. I told her not to worry that God would make a way for us to eat. I knew that we didn't have any bottles to take back to the store. I knew that I did not have any change in my usual hiding places. I knew that I didn't have any stash cash. I was not sure what we would do but I was trusting that the Lord would help us.

Most of the time my wife and/or I would walk over to the school and walk home with the boys. This time we both stayed home. As I would normally do I sat out on the porch and I would watch for them to come over the bridge. As soon as I saw them coming it hit me about supper. I had scoured the cupboards for food and we were pretty light. I still did not lose hope though that God would make a way for us. And now they are just a block away.

It was 3:14 and they were right on time....and so was the mail lady. As she walked up the stairs to give me my mail we chatted about the weather and soon she was down off the porch and on her way. Right behind her was the boys and all three came running up the stairs. All three came into the house and it was book bags flying and shoes being left in the front doorway. It only took Matthew about two seconds to inquire about grub. I told him that I was not sure but that we would be eating soon. I had no idea what we were going to eat but I still knew that God would make a way for us.

We had a half wall that separated the living room from the kitchen and when I walked in I just sat the mail on that wall. I really wasn't expecting anything but bills so I really didn't look that closely at the mail. My wife motioned me as was asking me about supper and I told her not to worry. I still had no idea what God had in store for us. As I got up to walk into the kitchen I stopped by and the thought came over me to check the mail. There were about eight or nine letters. As I looked them all over they were bills. The one however from our homeowners insurance company caught my eye because it wasn't in the usual billing envelope.

I only opened the one from my insurance company and it wasn't a bill it was just a letter. The letter went on to say that when we paid our premium last month that we over paid them by $8.37. They said that they usually just take that amount off of the next billing cycle but in this instance they sent with the letter a check for $8.37. I wanted to shout. That may not seem like a great deal of money but it was all we needed to get supper for that night.

Just across the river there is a mom and pop store that we shop at all the time. I was able to get milk, lunch meat, macaroni and cheese, and potato chips. We sat down to supper that night and we ate like kings. Yea, I know, sandwiches, chips, and mac and cheese are not usually on the menu at the palace. To me, my wife, and three little boys we were like royalty because the King of Kings and the Lord of Lords did not forsake us but kept His promise to always be there in our time of need. Even if it was only $8.37!

The David Painter CD

David Painter is a man from New Tazewell, Tennessee, and he is an extraordinary piano player and singer. He has dedicated his music to that of Christian praise and worship. From the time I first heard him play and sing I was hooked. Not only does he sing very well he does it as the Lord leads him. His talent mixed with the Spirit of God can bring a great blessing to your soul. He travels around to great distances to sing at churches, revival services, and homecomings. By his work and testimony I believe him to be a true man of God.

The first time that I heard him he was at Grape Missionary Baptist Church for their homecoming service. I was really blessed by his playing and singing. After the service I went to see if he had a CD that I could buy and he did not have any. The next time I saw him he didn't have any either. I was getting discouraged because I really wanted to have one of his CD's. He promised that when I saw him the next time that I could get one from him.

The next time that I saw him I forgot to get a CD from him. It seemed that I was never going to get the CD that I wanted. He sings a song called, **"Just a Place to Spend the Night"** and it tells about how that for God's people that die, that the grave is just a quick stopping over place for them on their journey to heaven. Every time I hear that song it reminds me of my mom and that is why it is so special to me. I kept wondering about the elusive CD that I may never get.

Time came and I finally got my CD and I was thrilled. I had it in my car and couldn't wait to get home and play it. My car has a CD player but I don't think it works right, so I decided that I would wait until I got it home to play it. I was tickled to death to have it. It was still in the plastic wrapper sitting right on my dashboard waiting to get played by me at home as soon as I got there........maybe?

My mom has the most unusual eating habits of anyone I know. She is a spontaneous eater with particular taste buds. She is not usually the type that you can just stop over and bring her a meatloaf and taters and corn. If she doesn't have a real hankering for it....forget it! I can ask her a hundred times what she is thinking that she may want for supper and I will get no answer. Came around 11pm and she will have me running across town to get her a pizza. I think that I have created a food monster because she knows that I will go just about anywhere to get her what she wants.

On this particular day I got a call from her and she told me to stop by and get her a certain meal from this place in Monroe. As I always do, I told her no problem and I rerouted to get there. While I didn't mind the detour I was still anxious to get home and peel open my long awaited CD from David. I called in her order and pulled in for the curb service. When I called in the order the girl told me it would be $12.87. I thought no problem because I knew that I had $20.00 on me. As I sat waiting for her to bring out the food it dawned on me that I had broken the $20.00 bill for something earlier and decided to count my cash. I had $13.00!

I panicked! I really hate it when people do not tip a wait person. That is so rude and insensitive and here I sit getting ready to do the thing I hate. I began to dig into my ashtray.....no coins. I started to dig in my seats.....no coins. I felt under my front seats frantically looking for a few dollars in change.....nothing. It was too late to change my order because she was going to be at my door at any minute. I cupped my face in my hands and thought, "Lord, what am I going to do now?" I tell this to people all the time; do not ask the Lord a question unless you are prepared to follow through with the answer that He gives you in return!

As I sat there with my face in my hands God said, "Give her your CD!" As I gritted my teeth I was reminded that I waited a very long time for this CD and on my way to listen to it I got side tracked. I began to bargain with God because I did not want to give something away that meant so much to me especially since I had not even opened it yet. God's presence was unrelenting as He continued to deal with my heart about giving the girl this CD in lieu of a tip. With the CD in my hand I waited for the door to open on the side of the restaurant.

After what seemed like a long time and I looked and here she came with a large bag of food. I did not have the words to say to her to explain my problem. She handed me the large bag and I handed her the $13.00. I thought, Lord please tell me what to say to this girl. As she counted the money I told her that there was only $13.00 dollars in her hand. I told her how that I did not have money for a tip and that I felt really bad. I told her how that tipping is one of my pet peeves with people that do not care. With a sheepish smile on her face she said, "That's ok thank you anyway." I really thought that she knew that I was sincere and not just blowing her off.

As she turned to walk away God said, "Give her the CD!" I called her back to the car and told her that I did not have any money to give her but I wanted her to have something more valuable than money. My first thought was that she would run back into the restaurant but she didn't.

As she made her way back to the driver's side window of my car I reached over on the dashboard and picked up that CD. As she looked at it in my hand I asked her if she had ever heard of David Painter from Tennessee. She told me no. I began to tell her how that I met him and how that I had listened to him sing and play the piano for the Lord. I told her how that I had waited and waited to finally get the CD that I was holding in my hand. I told her how that it had never been opened and had never been played. She just stood there and listened intently to me.

I told her that I feel that waitresses work very hard and deserve every penny that they get for helping people like me. I also told her that I was not trying to rip her off. What I really wanted her to know was that the message about the Lord that was contained in that every song on that CD was worth more than any amount of silver or gold. I told her that if she would take that CD and spend enough time listening to the words of each song that I believed that she would get blessed. I told her that the songs on this CD and the Lord to which they were dedicated to could provide her with a life changing event. She reached over and took it and told me thank you.

As she started to walk away I told her that if she did not really feel something deep in her heart after listening to the CD that she could do whatever that she wished with it. She told me thank you again and walked back into the restaurant. I do not know if she ever listened to that CD or not. I do know though that I did what God led me to do and have no regrets.

The Stolen Potatoes

Nestled in the woods in the small town of Harrison, Michigan sits a three room cabin. If my memory serves me correctly it was built in the late sixties or early seventies on a ten acre lot. It was relatively primitive but the memories and shared experiences of that little shack at the forked end of Vass Road are priceless to me. When I was a young boy we would travel up there for squirrel and deer hunting. In my minds eye I can see JB standing there at that gas stove cooking fried green tomatoes, macaroni and cheese, and his house special…..Ravioli!

September 15th of each year was a very special time because JB always wanted to be there for opening weekend of squirrel season. He would venture out and get five or six squirrels and come back and we would have a feast. Fried squirrel, fried potatoes, and his trademark squirrel gravy. My dad used to always say that when each of us got done eating the middle of the paper plate was gone for a reason. He said it was eaten to put hair on your chest. A volume of books could not do any justice to explain all of the wonderful trips and memories that I have at JB's Cabin.

As years passed by it was my turn to travel to Harrison with my boys and to continue the legacy of trips to JB's cabin. My neighbor Jeff Gruber was a real outdoorsman and when offered a trip to get to go to the infamous JB's cabin he readily jumped at the opportunity. So with my son Mitchell and Jeff we headed for a four day stay in the woods. It's about a four hour drive up there so it gave me plenty of time to share the many stories of the road with regard to the cabin.

We arrived and Jeff said it was everything that he imagined it would be. Oil stove, wooden floors and a manly outhouse for bathroom detail. He was delighted. It was in the fall of the year and the leaves looked awesome as their colors came into full bloom. Deer, squirrels, and blue jays dotted the landscape. After we got settled in I couldn't wait to show Jeff JB's Ravioli stash. He thought it was hilarious! The first night was awesome as we enjoyed the sights and sounds of the north woods.

Day two was just as nice! We went to town and got all of supplies and things that we needed for the rest of our trip. After we finished shopping I drove Jeff around to look at the many sights in Harrison. Our in-town visit ended with lunch at the Jack Pine Restaurant. I told Jeff that I had been eating at the Jack Pine for over 30 years and the food and atmosphere had not changed during that time. Once back at the cabin it was nap time!

Around 5pm we came out of our north-woods induced comas and decided that we would head out into the woods to romp around for a bit. As we walked around we discussed our supper plans and it was decided that steak and potatoes would be our meal. As we continued to walk through the woods we came to an opening about 150 feet by 150 feet. As I looked around I soon discovered that it was somebody's garden. This garden had everything in it. This garden had corn, beans, pumpkins, cucumbers, tomatoes, peppers, and the like. Somebody had taken a great deal of time and energy to put out a garden this nice.

Since it was towards the fall of the year I knew that the potatoes would be ready for "gravelling!" This technique is a southern practice whereby you just get down on the ground and "gravel" around the plant and get the top potatoes. I told Jeff about that term and he didn't know anything about it. I got down and dug with my fingers around the plant and out popped about six or eight new potatoes. They looked like golden nuggets to me. I showed him how that these potatoes are so fresh that you don't even have to peel them. The skin of the potato just rubs off in your hands.

Jeff, not wanting to be upstaged by me, got down on his hands and knees and tried it. The loose dirt at the top of the plant allows for the potatoes to just pop out. So he was surprised when in about ten seconds he too had about six or eight potatoes. He looked at me and said, "Let's eat!" He then picked up the potatoes that he had graveled and put them in his shirt. I picked up mine and held them in my shirt. As I stood there getting ready to leave with those "stolen potatoes" a really weird feeling came over me.

Since we had been walking for quite some time my son Mitchell asked me to carry him. At that time he was about 4 years old. So with my one hand holding my potatoes in my shirt I knelt down to pick him up with the other hand. As soon as I stood back up and took my first step I immediately realized something was dreadfully wrong!

I was wearing shorts so I felt them first on my legs as the stingers went deep into my skin. It wasn't but a second later and I heard Jeff screaming bloody murder. As I tried to take another step I felt the sharp needle pricks in my thighs and could feel something crawling under my shorts. I looked over and Jeff was beating the air out of his shirt and fighting a losing battle with our new found friends. Next I felt as if I was getting about ten shots at the doctors, five in each arm. My back was also getting pummeled and I soon felt them on my neck. Jeff was now down on the ground and he was rolling around as if his clothes were on fire. He just kept screaming and smacking his arms and legs. I now was getting stung in the face.

By now I could feel the hornets as they were in my hair and stinging me on my face, neck, back, legs, arms, and head. I dropped my potatoes and tried to swat at them but this just brought out their furry even more. I then realized that I was holding Mitchell and I got really scared because I did not know how badly that he was getting stung. I knew that I couldn't drop to the ground because again I thought that if I did Mitchell would get hurt. We were in dire straights to say the least.

Finally I looked over and Jeff was able to run away and soon I watched as he was pulling the last of the hornets off and out of his body. All told he got stung about 20 times. He looked peppered. By now the attack had subsided for the most part and I was really hurting. By my last count I looked and I too got stung more than 20 times. I was hit from my ankles to the top of my head. I thought for sure that if one or both of us had an allergic reaction that we would be in big trouble.

Even though I was in real pain my main concern was Mitchell. I was away now from the hornets and I dropped down on my knees and started to look him over. He was not scared at all. He was not crying at all. He had not one sting mark on him. He did not have even one remnant of any of those hornets on his clothes or in his hair. It looked like there was a thousand or more of those hornets all around us as we fought with them and not one of them stung him.

As Jeff and I sat there licking our wounds he couldn't believe that Mitchell had not been touched. He said, "With all of those hornets how is it possible that Mitchell never got touched?" The thought came over me to tell Jeff this, "Mitchell didn't steal that man's potatoes…..we did!" I told Jeff that we were wrong for taking them without permission. I told Jeff that I had no idea whose garden that was because it was literally out in the middle of the woods. I told him that I wished that I could find the man and apologize for taking them. We sat the potatoes back on the plants where we graveled them and walked back to the cabin.

As we walked I carried Mitchell and he asked me why that Jeff and I were screaming and crying. I told him that I took something from somebody without permission and even though the man that owned the garden never saw us…. God did! I told him that daddy knew better than to take them and that I was wrong. From that day until now when I think about gravelling potatoes I know that God wants me to dig only my own and that by His endless miracles a four year old boy did not have to pay for his daddy's mistake!

Bagheera

My youngest son Mark came running into the house to tell me how that the Sortor's cat was going to have kittens. I could see by the glitter in his eyes that he was up to something. He immediately asked me if he could have one. I told him that I didn't care if he had one and if it was ok with his mom that he was golden. His mom gave her blessing and Mark was on cloud nine. He was so intent on getting one of these cats that he went over every morning before school to check on the expecting mother and every night after school did the same. He was counting the days like an expecting father.

About two or three times a week Mark gave me an interrogation about my continued willingness for him to have a kitten. No matter how much I assured him his patience grew weaker by the day. He told me that it could be any day now and that they would be born. He kept a daily vigil over the mother. He told me that the Sortor girls had told him that he gets first pick when they are born. He was good with everything that they had to say except for the six week time that the babies had to be with their mother.

We lived across that street from the Sortor family. Rex and Wilma were the mom and dad and they had three daughters. Rachel, Amanda, and Sarah were the girls and they shared in Mark's enthusiasm for the upcoming addition to their family. They told Mark that the mommy cat had a bed in the garage and that is where the kittens would be born. They also told Mark that he could come over any time night or day to visit during the six week period that the babies had to be with their mom.

That morning arrived but in a manner in which none of us would have thought. Mark had gotten up that morning for school and as he sat in the kitchen eating breakfast he said that he could hear kittens meowing. I laughed and told him for the millionth time that he could have a kitten as soon as they were born. He said, "But dad you don't understand I can hear them." Mark was setting at the end of the table with his back to the landing that went out into our garage that was attached to our house. From that location Mark was only about five feet from the garage door opening.

Again I just laughed it off as pre-birth jitters. Mark yelled to me again and told me that he could hear the kittens. I ignored him. When one of his brothers came and sat down at the table to eat Mark said, "Be real quiet and listen." This time both boys came running into my bedroom and told me that they could hear the kittens. I knew then that they both weren't senile!

As I made my way to the kitchen landing all three boys and I stood there very quiet and gave ear. Sure enough we could all hear kittens meowing and it sounded like it was coming from right behind the door leading into our garage. I told the boys that if they were there that we had to be very careful not to scare the mom. I told them that we would go outside and come in from the front so that the mother could see us and hopefully not get scared. Mark and his brothers were going out of their minds. We knew it was kittens but we were not sure if it was the Sortor's cat.

We all scampered outside and came in through the big door and sure enough hidden under the work bench on some old blankets was the Sortor's cat and she never paid us no mind. I told the boys that we could try and get close to see the babies bearing in mind that we did not want to scare her. As we looked the proud momma was resting and the babies were trying to eat. I told the boys that we needed to back out and leave her alone. Mark was insistent that he was not going to school but he finally relented and went. I told him that they would be ok until he got home. He was all smiles!

As soon as I heard the air brakes on the bus I knew that Mark was home. He beat a path to the garage only to find that his dreams of a kitten were dashed. The mother and all of the babies were gone. He just cried and cried. There was no consoling him. All of a sudden one of the Sortor girls came running over and told us that all of the kittens were in their barn safe and sound. Mark ran like his hair was on fire to see them. When he got there they were cleaned and trying to crawl around. He was in seventh heaven.

Like a kid in a candy store he just sat there and gazed at them. A few were yellow, a couple was grey, one was white like her mother and there was only one solid black one. He chose the black one. The Sortor girls assured him that the black one was his. He was elated. As we sat there looking at them I asked him if he had a name and he said yes. Mark said, "Dad I am going to call him Bagheera like the black cat from the movie Jungle Book." I looked at him and said, "Bagheera it is!"

Six weeks is not a long time if you are counting interest on your money but to a seven year old boy that time span is eternity plus twenty years. Every morning he was up early before school and would go visit. As soon as his feet hit the ground when he got off that bus after school he was running toward their garage. I told Mark that he could visit but not to try to do too much while the babies are still little. Mark was always a good boy but his desire was to be with his cat. I told him that the mother is very protective of them because they can't take care of themselves.

As the sixth week approached Mark was ready to move his little kitten to its new home. I still remember the day that he walked that kitten home he could not have been more proud than he was that day. Bagheera was to be an inside cat because it is much safer that way. Cats that stay inside can live nearly twenty years. An outside cat lives an average of about eighteen months. So Mark done up a litter box and got a food and water dish and blankets. He was bound and determined to give this cat the royal treatment.

Bagheera lived with Mark all through grade school, junior high, and high school. They were inseparable until he left to go to the Marine Corps. This few short years would be the only time that they would not be together. Mark would go to sleep and when I would check on him Bagheera would be right in the bed with him. It would be quite amusing at times because that cat would lie around Marks neck and sleep. He would look like a neck warmer! This is how close that they were.

Bagheera was an indoor cat but he enjoyed his time outside rousting about in the neighborhood. His trumps and triumphs were usually short lived because he was neutered and had no front claws. This put him at a distinct disadvantage because when he would go romancing all he could do was wish and when it came to fighting the other stray cats he usually lost. He wouldn't stay out for long and there he would be sitting in his same spot on the porch waiting for the doorman to let him in. One night that all changed!

I went to the door and he was not there and that was unusual. The next morning I figured that I would get up and he would be sitting on the front porch....ticked off.....but he wasn't. After about a day and a half I knew something was wrong. I started looking around for him to no avail. I was not sure what to do. A check at the local pet shelter and County Animal Control failed to provide me with any info on the elusive Bagheera. Since Mark was not living at home due to his work in the military he had no idea that he was gone. I dreaded calling him.

Like a missing son I wondered about where he could be. I thought several times that he may have been hit by a car and ran off and died somewhere. I wondered if someone just took him in because he was such an awesome feline. The search for him went on for weeks and weeks. My heart was broken and I knew that time would draw near that I would have to tell Mark. That part of this whole chapter about the endless miracles of God bothered me the most. As the previous chapters pointed out, this was not just about a kid who wondered upon a lot of kittens and picked one out of the crowd. This was about a little boy who chose a soul mate friend.

As the days and weeks drug on my hope was fading that I would ever see Begheera again. I basically did the one thing that I do when all hope in my own efforts begin to fail.....I talked to God about it. I tell people all the time that God really does care about them and the things that they care about. He sits daily on His throne wanting to hear from us. He wants us to seek Him in the good times and the bad. He wants us to have communion with Him daily. People tell me that He does not care about us....yes He does! People tell me that He does not care about our home....yes He does! People tell me that He does not care about our animals and pets....yes He does! Anything that is dear to our heart; God really cares about us and whatever that it may be that we love or have need of.

That night as I went to bed I told God, "Please Lord don't let it end this way!" My thoughts ran rampant through the night as I thought about all of the history that Mark and Bagheera had. I thought about how saddened that he would be if I told him that his favorite friend was gone. My heart was truly broken and I sought God in sincerity. In my room I felt that wonderful peace that God gives as we seek Him and His help.

The next morning I got up with the assurance that God and I had connected during the midnight hour about Bagheera. I was upstairs and when I came down the stairs I just felt the Lord leading me to go out onto the porch so I did. As I stepped out onto the porch I looked to the north and about two houses down I noticed that same familiar cat waltzing down the sidewalk heading for home.

I thought I saw a sheepish grin on his face (not really) and I know that my eyes pooled up with tears. As I stood on the porch he made his way up the steps, stopped by just long enough for me to get in a quick rub on my legs, and then he stopped at the door. As I stood there I began to praise God for all of His wonderful love and mercy. Bagheera just looked back over his shoulder and as he looked intently at me his eyes were saying, "I'm home now and I would really like something to eat!" God's endless love!

Bert Laney

I got word that a family friend had died and I wanted to go to the funeral home and pay my respects. As I walked up to the back door of the funeral home I read the names of the people who were there for funeral services and I realized that I was close friends with all three. That thought was accepted with mixed emotions! As I made my way in I stopped in the one parlor and visited with the family for a short time. From there it was off to the next parlor for the second family friend. I sat with that family for a time and then it was off to the other parlor to see my friend Mr. Bert Laney.

The second parlor and third parlor were separated by a short narrow hallway and in that hallway was an office. This small office was there for a place for funeral home staff to meet with family or for clergy members to sit while preparing for the service. As I walked by that room the door was open and I saw a long time friend and church Pastor Reverend Fred Cornelius. I stuck my head in the door and with a smile he called out to me and said hello. I asked him who he was conducting a service for and he said, Mr. Laney. My heart was overjoyed!

As I stood there we chatted for just a moment but I sensed right away that something was just not right. I then asked Brother Fred if everything was ok and he said no. I asked him what was wrong. He told me that he did not know Mr. Laney and that it was hard for him to conduct a funeral service for someone that he didn't know and if he was not sure if they were a Christian. As my skin crawled all over my body I asked him if he had time for a true story about Mr. Laney. He opened the door the rest of the way and offered me a chair. As he sat and listened intently I told him the story of Bert Laney!

During the time that I was about eight until I was about eleven I lived in a small dead end subdivision named Evergreen Acres. The sub consisted of six short streets that were connected by a large horseshoe shaped main road. We lived on Norway, the last street in the subdivision. Kitty corner to our house lived a couple and their name was Bert and Shirley Laney. Mrs. Laney was a kind hearted woman that loved everybody and was always laughing and smiling. Bert was a retired automobile factory worker who stayed drunk most of the time. Everybody in the neighborhood loved them because they were loveable people. My mom used to tell me that Bert Laney never did any harm to anyone but to himself. In all the years I knew him I found that fact to be very true.

Bert was always telling stories about every topic possible in life. If a neighbor grew a five pound tomato, he grew one that weighed six. If your Thanksgiving turkey weighed in at forty pounds, his weighed fifty. If your car got twenty miles to the gallon, his got thirty. His stories were never ending. He was never a bother or hurt to anyone though. For all of those years that we lived on that street Mr. Laney never stopped telling his stories.

Time would come that I would move with my mom and dad down to a little township location called LaSalle, Michigan. Even though we were no longer neighbors I kept in contact with them. As I got older I thought much about Bert and how that my Aunt Mary Lee that lived across the street from them would talk to him about the Lord. He would usually just shrug it off and I never really thought that he worried much about his salvation. I have sat under the preaching of God's word long enough to know that when Jesus said that we had to born again to see the kingdom of heaven....He meant it. Never seeing Bert go to church and/or give a testimony about accepting the Lord as his personal savior bothered me for years.

As I got older I started talking to him about the Lord and invited him to come to church. He was a kind gent so he usually made an excuse that he was too busy. I'm not a Bible thumper but I am one that will invite people to learn about the Lord. Even though that I had invited him many times over the years he never darkened the door of the church. Since the church is only three streets from Norway Drive where he lived I told him he could even walk. I never saw him there!

The years passed by and one day my mom told me that Bert was really sick and that I should go and see him. I drove over to that same old house and Shirley answered the door. She told me that he was really sick but he would love to see me. Even though he was bad he knew it was me. The room was dark with only a dim table lamp in the room for light. As I stood there my heart was breaking because he looked like that he could pass away at any moment. He invited me to sit down and we started to chat about the old days. Even though his voice was weak he still came out with his natural charm.

After what seemed like hours of story telling I knew that the time had come for me to ask him the question that I came over for in the first place. I wanted to know if all was well with his soul. I said, "Bert, I told my mom that I wanted to come and see you because I wanted to ask you a very important question." He told me to go ahead with my question. The power of God was so thick in that room it could have been cut with a chain saw. I looked intently at him and asked, "Are you saved and ready to go?"

Through that dim light I looked at him as he turned his head towards me and said, "A couple of weeks ago I was lying here in the bed and I was asleep and all of a sudden I felt the presence of someone in my room. I never saw the face of who that it was but they told me to get up and to walk with them. I got up and immediately I was now walking down a long dirt road and it was dark out. I could feel that person next to me as we walked down this road. The man next to me never said a word. As we continued to walk I looked up ahead of me and I started to see an orange and red glow coming up from a large hole at the edge of the road. As we got closer I could feel waves of the heat hitting me in the face."

"As I got up closer to the edge we were standing on a cliff and the man said look down there as he pointed over the edge. As I took a few more steps I got right to the edge of that cliff and I looked down. I couldn't see their faces but I could see people languishing down in that hole as they tried to get out. I could hear them screaming and begging God to let them out. As I stood there in horror I would feel a blast of that heat hit me in the face and it would take my breath away. Just then I could feel that man that had walked with me as he moved up next to me. As we both stood there I could not even comprehend what I was seeing and hearing."

"After a few minutes of just standing there and listening to those people crying and screaming the man standing next to me said, "If you do not get saved and accept the Lord as your personal savior this is where you will spend eternity." And I woke up!

Bert went on to say as he opened up his eyes that he was not on the edge of that cliff anymore but was in his bed. He said that he never saw the face of the man that walked with him but was sure that it must have been an angel or the Lord Himself. He said that he had never known fear in all of his life like he was feeling right at that moment He said that he began to cry out on the Lord and told Him that he was lost and on his way to that fiery pit of hell and was sure that he did not want to go there. He said that he asked the Lord to save him so that he could escape that awful place.

As he laid there with tears in his eyes Bert said that the spirit of the Lord came into his bedroom in a mighty way. He said that he had never felt a peace come over him like that in all of his life. He said I know now for a fact that the Lord saved me that night and I now have a home in heaven. I wanted to jump up and down and shout for joy. As we finished our visit I could tell that there had been a change in him. I come on business for the Lord to find out if this old friend and neighbor of mine was ready to meet the Lord in a free pardon of sin. After that night I didn't worry anymore!

As Brother Fred sat there I could see the joy and glitter in his eyes as he took in every word of this wonderful testimony about the man that he would soon be preaching over. He told me that it was a great relief to know that Mr. Laney had made a profession of faith. I told Brother Fred that he should have been there with me a couple of weeks ago when Bert told me his testimony first hand. I stood up and gave Brother Fred a hug and told him that I would be praying for him while he conducted the funeral service for Mr. Laney. God is so good!

"Run Into Someone"

Often times when I wake up in the morning I will ask God to let me, "Run into Someone" today that may need a helping hand, a kind word, or just whatever that they may have need of. On this one particular afternoon I was sitting in the intersection of Telegraph and South Custer (M-50) Roads when all of a sudden a car slammed into the back of my car. As I looked in my rear view mirror I noticed as this female driver just dropped her head. I wasn't hurt but I sure felt the impact of that collision.

My car is a licensed emergency vehicle equipped with emergency lights and a siren. Since I was not willing to be out in one of Monroe's busiest intersections without some protection, I activated my red beacon and flashers. As I looked back again I saw the driver again drop her head and this time she was shaking it. I stepped out of my car and she got out of her car and as she walked up I asked her if she was ok. With a sheepish grin she told me that she should be asking me if I was ok. I assured her that I was fine.

As we checked out the minor damage to my vehicle the topic came up for the need for a police report. She said she would rather not and I concurred. As we chatted I asked her if I could share a story with her. She told me to say on! I told her about how I would often inquire with God about a desire to "Run into Someone" during my day that may have a need in their life. As soon as I said this tears pooled up in her eyes. I then told her that as it turned out, she ran into me!

I told her that I did not believe for one minute that this accident was an accident at all. I told her that God ordained our meeting that day in the middle of the busiest intersection of Monroe for a reason. She began to cry. I then asked her to tell me what was going on in her world thus the reason we were brought together. She then told me that she was home and had just received a call from our local hospital that her mother-in-law, who was a patient in the ICU, had just taken a serious turn for the worse and the family should try to get there as soon as possible. I looked intently at her and told her that I now knew the reason for her running into me.

I told her we should pray for her mother-in-law. Right smack dab in this busy intersection one would think that the noise would be very loud. Another might think that other drivers would be angry trying to drive around us. Some may even consider that people would be yelling at us to move. As God knows my heart, I don't think either one of us heard any sounds of that busy intersection at all. Essentially, we were in our own world as the Lord was performing another miracle.

I told her I would continue to remember her mother-in-law in prayer assuring her that God loved her and that He cared about her. She hugged me and walked back to her car. As we drove away I wondered how she felt about the encounter. I don't believe for a minute this was a chance happening at all. Simply, this was another opportunity for God to show His divine mercy and love to someone in need! Endless Miracles of God.

Fireman Dave McFadden
September 1977 to Present

PARAMEDIC INSTRUCTOR/COORDINATOR-LIFE SUPPORT TRAINING INSTITUTE
ASSOCIATE OF SCIENCE-MONROE COUNTY COMMUNITY COLLEGE
INSTRUCTOR-MICHIGAN FIREFIGHTER'S TRAINING COUNCIL
FIRE OFFICER III-MACOMB COUNTY COMMUNITY COLLEGE
FIRE OFFICER II-MACOMB COUNTY COMMUNITY COLLEGE
FIRE OFFICER I-MACOMB COUNTY COMMUNITY COLLEGE
PARAMEDIC SCHOOL-WASHTENAW CO. COMM. COLLEGE
VEHICLE ARSON/FIRE SCHOOL-MICHIGAN STATE POLICE
EMT SCHOOL-MONROE COUNTY COMMUNITY COLLEGE
FIRE SCIENCE DEGREE-OWENS COMMUNITY COLLEGE
MEDICAL ASSISTANT PROGRAM-MASON HIGH SCHOOL
ADVANCED CARDIAC LIFE SUPPORT INSTRUCTOR-AHA
PEDIATRIC ADVANCED LIFE SUPPORT PROVIDER-AHA
BASIC ARSON/FIRE SCHOOL-MICHIGAN STATE POLICE
BASIC ROPE RESCUE SCHOOL-TOLEDO FIRE DIVISION
CRASH FIRE RESCUE SCHOOL-TOLEDO FIRE DIVISION
BACHELOR OF SCIENCE-SIENA HEIGHTS UNIVERSITY
ADVANCED CARDIAC LIFE SUPPORT PROVIDER-AHA
ATHLETIC TRAINER-MASON SENIOR HIGH SCHOOL
FIREFIGHTER II-FRENCHTOWN FIRE DEPARTMENT
FIREFIGHTER I-FRENCHTOWN FIRE DEPARTMENT
MERCHANT MARINE FF SCHOOL-TOLEDO MIRIAD
BASIC CARDIAC LIFE SUPPORT INSTRUCTOR-AHA
PRE-HOSPITAL TRAUMA LIFE SUPPORT COURSE
BASIC CARDIAC LIFE SUPPORT PROVIDER-AHA
TERRORISM AWARENESS INSTRUCTOR-FEMA
MONTANA TRAUMA LIFE SUPPORT COURSE
GRADUATE-MASON SENIOR HIGH SCHOOL
RESCUE/RECOVERY SCUBA DIVER
HAZ-MAT OPERATIONAL LEVEL
HAZ-MAT AWARENESS LEVEL
TOLEDO FIRE ACADEMY
NIMS 100-800 FEMA

My Cup Runneth Over!
(Psalms 23:5)

Made in the USA
Columbia, SC
15 August 2017